Blackburn Rovers, An A–Z

by Dean Hayes

D1344477

Palatine Books, 1993

Blackburn Rovers, An A–Z

by Dean Hayes

Palatine Books, 1993

Blackburn Rovers, An A–Z
by Dean Hayes
Published by Palatine Books, an imprint of Carnegie Publishing Ltd, 18 Maynard Street,
Preston
Text copyright © Dean Hayes, 1993
Illustrations copyright ©, see List of Illustrations
Typeset by Carnegie Publishing, Preston
Printed in the UK by T. Snape & Co., Preston
British Library Cataloguing-in-Publication Data
A CIP catalogue record for this book is available from the British Library
ISBN 1-874181-10-1

*This book is dedicated to Blackburn fans everywhere,
but especially to the many children and parents at Brindle St James School
near Chorley who support the Rovers.*

Contents

Abandoned Matches

AN ABANDONED MATCH may be defined as one that is called off by the referee, *whilst it is in progress*, because conditions do not permit it to be completed.

Generally speaking, far fewer matches are abandoned in modern times because if there is some doubt about the ability to play the full game the match is more likely to be postponed.

When Rovers met Huddersfield Town on New Year's Day 1926, the weather was filthy—torrential rain and a bitterly cold wind. The sequel to this was the collapse of the referee and his removal from the field on the back of the Rovers' trainer and the ultimate abandonment of the game after forty-two minutes by the man who took his place, Mr H. Brewster of Burnley. Most people were under the impression that the first half had run its normal course and it was perhaps not surprising in view of the confusion caused by the stoppage when the referee, Mr W. G. Forshaw of Liverpool, had to leave the scene of action. There were some rumours at the time that the abandonment followed the retirement of the teams but the fact was, of course, that Mr Brewster was alone in making his decision.

Accrington

A DIFFERENT CLUB from the Accrington Stanley team which joined the league in 1921, Accrington were founder members of the Football League in 1888 and resigned in 1893 after being relegated to the Second Division. They are the only founder members of the league no longer in membership.

It was Accrington who opposed Rovers on their debut in the Football League. Several times in arrears, the Rovers hit back to draw the game at five goals each. The league was all but finished in January,

when Rovers won 2–0 at Accrington, such was the organisation of the fixtures. Though Rovers were almost certain to finish in the top four, victory had long been destined for Preston. This left the cup, where Accrington again provided the opposition. They were beaten 5–0 after a draw away from home.

Terry Gennoe: Blackburn Rovers' oldest goalkeeper, who played his last match for the club at the grand old age of 37 years, 162 days.

The clubs met on ten occasions in the Football League, with Rovers' only defeat being 1–0 at Accrington, on 27 January 1892.

Age

Youngest: THE YOUNG-EST PLAYER to appear in a Football League fixture for Blackburn Rovers was *Harry Dennison*, who made his league debut in the match against Bristol City (home 2–0) on 8 April 1911, when he was just 16 years and 155 days old. He was a schoolboy at Blackburn Grammar School when he played for the first team. He was young and looked it. At a reserve game,

the gateman refused to believe he was playing and refused to let him through.

Oldest: THE OLDEST PLAYER to line up in a Rovers' first team in the Football League was *Bob Crompton*. Bob was 40 years and 151 days when he last turned out for the club, at Bradford (2–5) on 23 February 1920.

The oldest goalkeeper in Rovers' history is *Terry Gennoe*, who played his last match against Bristol City at Ashton Gate (2–4) on 25 August 1990 at the age of 37 years and 162 days.

Aircraft

ON WEDNESDAY 22 May 1991, a banner-trailing aircraft flew over Turf Moor during Burnley's crucial play-off match against Torquay United. The cruel message was: 'Staying Down 4 Ever, Luv Rovers, Ha Ha Ha.'

Aldershot

IN MARCH 1992 the liquidator who had been called in to supervise the winding up of the 'Shots' confirmed to the Football League that no offers had been received for the Fourth Division club.

Rovers met Aldershot for the first time on 24 April 1974 in the Third Division, going down 1–2 at Ewood. The return match three days later saw Rovers beaten by four clear goals. The following season saw the last two matches that the clubs were involved in against each other. Rovers gained revenge by beating the 'Shots' 2–0 at Ewood and drawing 1–1 at the Recreation Ground.

The Rovers never won in the league at Aldershot and of course now, due to their folding, never will!

Alexandra Meadows

FOR THE FIRST HALF of the 1877–8 season, the Rovers played their 'home' matches on the Pleasington cricket ground, but by Christmas 1877 they had rented the Alexandra Meadows. This was also a cricket ground which was enclosed and had the luxury of a pavilion.

By now the status of the club was such that on 2 January 1879 they entertained the Partick team in the first match at their new home. The Rovers won 2–1 with A. N. Hornby, then a great international rugby player, playing for the home side and Fergie Suter, one of the finest backs in the country, for Partick.

During the club's stay at the Alexandra Meadows, which was for less than two years, they entered the FA Cup for the first time and reached the third round.

The club also had a taste of floodlit football when Darwen were the visitors on 4 November 1879. There was a no more competitive match than that staged at Alexandra Meadows on 27 November 1880 when again Darwen were the opponents. An estimated crowd of 10,000 had crammed into the ground and as well as packing the grandstand, twenty lorries provided raised viewing platforms. During the first half both sides scored a goal, and on two occasions the crowd broke through the ropes. Eight minutes into the second half, Marshall of Darwen was robbed of the ball, whereupon he grabbed his adversary and threw him down near the touchline. This was the signal for a mass pitch invasion, and the game had to be abandoned!

On 26 February the club were honoured with an international match—England *v.* Wales—being staged at their headquarters. The last match at Alexandra Meadows was probably that against Notts Forest on 12 March before a crowd of over 4,000.

American Soccer League

IN JUNE 1964 the Rovers were invited to represent England in the New York International Tournament, a competition in which West Ham

United had distinguished themselves. Unfortunately, the club had not recovered the poise of the previous season and lost twice to Hearts and once each to Lanerossi and Werder Bremen. Its only successes were a win and a draw against Bahia of Brazil.

Results		
Bahia	Los Angeles	Drew 1–1
Werder Bremen	Los Angeles	Lost 2–3
Lanerossi	New York	Lost 1–3
Bahia	New York	Won 3–1
Hearts	New York	Lost 0–2
Hearts	New York	Lost 0–1

Anglo-Scottish Cup

THE ANGLO-SCOTTISH CUP was inaugurated in 1975–6 following the withdrawal of Texaco from the competition of that name. The first winners were Middlesbrough who defeated Fulham 1–0 on aggregate after the two legs were completed. The Rovers reached the quarter-finals and lost in that round to Scottish Premier League side Motherwell 2–1 in a two-legged game.

The Rovers reached the quarter-final stage again in 1977–8 only to lose 3–1 to Hibernian over the two legs.

In fact, these two quarter-final clashes were the only occasions on which Rovers met clubs from across the border. Playing in the competition until 1980–1, Rovers' record against English clubs was as follows:

P	W	D	L	F	A
18	9	5	4	26	20

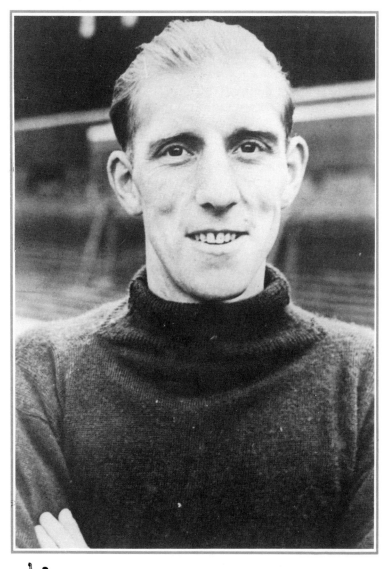

Reg Elvy: the only Blackburn Rovers player to make over one hundred consecutive League appearances immediately after his debut for the Club on 10 November 1951.

Appearances

THE PLAYERS with the highest number of appearances for Blackburn Rovers are as follows:

	Football League	FA and Football League Cups	Total
Derek Fazackerley	593 (3)	78	671 (3)
Ronnie Clayton	579 (2)	84	663 (2)
Bob Crompton	530	46	576
Simon Garner	455 (29)	56 (7)	511 (36)
Bryan Douglas	438	64 (1)	502 (1)
Bill Eckersley	406	26	432
William Bradshaw	386	39	425
Stuart Metcalfe	376 (11)	45 (2)	421 (13)
Glenn Keeley	365 (5)	42 (1)	407 (6)
Harry Healless	360	36	396

Consecutive appearances

Only Reg Elvy has ever made over one hundred consecutive League apperances for the Club, immediately following his debut in November 1951.

Reg Elvy: 152 appearances
Debut 10 November 1951 *v.* Cardiff City (home 0–1).

Six players have made over one hundred consecutive appearances at any time during their careers with Blackburn Rovers.

Walter Crook: 208 appearances
From 22 December 1934 to 7 December 1946.

John Bruton: 115 appearances
From 22 November 1930 to 3 February 1934.

Derek Fazackerley: 112 appearances
   From 29 January 1972 to 1 May 1974

Roger Jones: 107 appearances
   From 16 October 1971 to 3 February 1974

Ron Suart: 106 appearances
   From 3 November 1951 to 11 December 1954

Glenn Keeley: 101 appearances
   From 12 January 1980 to 24 April 1982.

Attendances at Ewood Park

Attendances figures at home provide some interesting statistics:

Opponents	Date	Competition	Attendance
Individual matches: highest in the Football League			
Preston North End	26 December 1921	Division One	52,656
Burnley	1 January 1914	Division One	48,000
Preston North End	4 October 1947	Division One	46,874
Leicester City	16 April 1954	Division Two	45,521
Preston North End	4 November 1950	Division Two	44,612
Wolverhampton W's	13 September 1958	Division One	43,192
Preston North End	7 April 1950	Division Two	42,891
Burnley	16 October 1926	Division One	42,000
Tottenham Hotspur	30 August 1958	Division One	41,830
Liverpool	22 February 1958	Division Two	41,789
Lowest attendance (since the First World War)			
Wimbledon	8 October 1985	League Cup Round 2	2,161
Wigan Athletic	2 September 1986	League Cup Round 1	2,831

Birmingham City	2 April 1925	Division One	3,000
Aston Villa	29 April 1933	Division One	3,624
Willington	3 December 1973	FA Cup Round 1 (replay)	4,025
Brentford	27 October 1982	League Cup Round 2	4,137
Brentford	27 September 1988	League Cup Round 2	4,606
Barrow	14 August 1966	League Cup Round 2	4,655

Other games at Ewood Park

Bolton Wanderers	2 March 1929	FA Cup Round 6	61,783
Blackpool	4 March 1925	FA Cup Round 4	60,011
Huddersfield Town	9 March 1939	FA Cup Round 6 (replay)	54,400
Burnley	16 March 1960	FA Cup Round 6 (replay)	53,839
Everton	25 January 1930	FA Cup Round 4	53,000
Burnley	8 March 1952	FA Cup Round 6	52,920
Liverpool	7 January 1950	FA Cup Round 3	52,468
Blackpool	30 January 1960	FA Cup Round 4	51,223
West Brom. Albion	23 February 1952	FA Cup Round 5	51,177
Liverpool	1 March 1958	FA Cup Round 6	51,000

Blackburn Rovers' average home attendances over the last ten years have been as follows:

1983–4	7,622	1988–9	8,891
1984–5	9,641	1989–90	9,624
1985–6	5,826	1990–1	8,126
1986–7	6,772	1991–2	13,288
1987–8	9,502	1992–3	16,141

Away

Opponents	Date	Competition	Score

Best away wins

Opponents	Date	Competition	Score
West Ham United	26 December 1963	Division One	8–2
Bootle	15 February 1890	FA Cup Round 2	7–0
Burnley	3 November 1888	Football League	7–1
Newcastle United	9 September 1925	Division One	7–1
Sheffield United	3 March 1930	Division One	7–5
Burnley	18 October 1890	Football League	6–1

Worst away defeats

Opponents	Date	Competition	Score
Arsenal	25 February 1933	Division One	0–8
Lincoln City	29 August 1953	Division Two	0–8
Wolverhampton W's	30 November 1935	Division One	1–8
West Brom. Albion	18 January 1936	Division One	1–8
Manchester City	8 November 1919	Division One	2–8
Derby County	6 September 1890	Football League	5–8
Sheffield United	9 January 1897	Division One	0–7
Everton	14 October 1933	Division One	1–7
Bradford	29 January 1938	Division Two	1–7
Shrewsbury Town	2 October 1971	Division Three	1–7
Sunderland	21 September 1935	Division One	2–7
Fulham	26 December 1956	Division Two	2–7
Luton Town	27 November 1954	Division Two	3–7

Highest scoring away draws

Opponents	Date	Competition	Score
Birmingham City	24 April 1965	Division One	5–5
Everton	21 November 1908	Division One	4–4

Most away wins in a season: 12 in 1979–80 (Division Three)

Fewest away wins in a season: 1 in 1899–1900 (Division One)

1 in 1910–11	(Division One)
1 in 1937–8	(Division Two)
1 in 1970–1	(Division Two)
Most away defeats in a season: 17 in 1933–4	(Division One)
Fewest away defeats in a season: 4 in 1908–9	(Division One)
Most away goals in a season: 45 in 1963–4	(Division One)
Fewest away goals in a season: 8 in 1896–7	(Division One)

Balls

WHEN ROVERS entertained Burnley at Ewood on 2 September 1944, three balls were used.

Potts, the Burnley inside-right, struck a shot into the Blackburn net with such force that when the ball—an ordinary brown one—was centred for the re-start, the referee called for a fresh one. One of a vivid yellow colour was produced, and when this had been used for five minutes, the referee called for another. This time a black one was forthcoming.

If the game, which Rovers lost 0–2, had gone on long enough, they might have gone through a complete set of snooker balls!

Jackie Bestall

JACKIE BESTALL was responsible for signing Ronnie Clayton and Bryan Douglas, so Blackburn soccer-lovers will always be in his debt, but it was during his charge that Rovers came very close to relegation.

As a player, Bestall had enjoyed a very successful career with Grimsby Town. On retiring in June 1938, he moved to Birmingham in a coaching and scouting capacity. It was at the end of the war when he moved into football management, taking over the reins at Doncaster

Rovers. A successful spell at Belle Vue ended in April 1949 and two months later he arrived at Ewood Park.

Bestall set about reviving Rovers' fortunes and though he was keen to encourage youth in the shape of Clayton and Douglas, he also strengthened the team with more experienced players like Elvy, Kelly, Quigley, Briggs and Smith. However, success continued to elude Blackburn and an appearance in the FA Cup semi-final of 1951 was little compensation for a club whose rightful place was surely the First Division.

Bestall's problems increased during the 1952–3 season and were not helped by rumours of disputes between manager and players. In May 1953 it was announced that Bestall had decided it would be in everyone's best interests if he left. Although the little man had no plans for his future, the parting was an amicable one.

Best Starts

THE ROVERS have been unbeaten for the first ten games of a league season on two occasions—1913–14 and 1989–90.

In 1913–14, when the club won the First Division Championship, they started the season with five straight wins before being held to a 1–1 draw at Sheffield United. The records of those two best starts are:

	P	W	D	L	F	A	Pts
1913–14	10	7	3	0	29	10	17
1989–90	10	4	6	0	18	9	18

Blackburn Olympic

BLACKBURN OLYMPIC came into existence about three years after Blackburn Rovers had been founded. The Olympic arose through the

amalgamation of two minor clubs, Black Star and James Street, early in 1878.

They were very largely working men who had formed this club in opposition to the Rovers, then regarded as the 'gentlemen's club' in Blackburn. In 1878–9 they never lost a match, and when the East Lancashire Charity Cup was first put up in 1881–2, Olympic won it.

They became so strong that in 1882–3 they reached the FA Cup final and beat Old Etonians by 2–1, this being the first club to bring the cup away from London into the provinces. The following season they were beaten in the semi-final by Queen's Park and then, as professionalism grew, they gradually declined. They were over-shadowed by the Rovers and although the two teams played each other until 1889, Blackburn, which could not support two professional teams, turned more and more to the Rovers.

The short but outstanding career of Blackburn Olympic, a team of nine Lancashire working men and two Yorkshiremen, was a triumph for democracy!

Bolton Wanderers

THERE ARE SOME particularly vivid memories of past encounters between Rovers and their rivals, Bolton Wanderers.

The two clubs were both among the original members of the Football League and met for the first time on 8 December 1888, drawing 4–4 at Blackburn. On 7 January 1928 the Wanderers beat Rovers 6–1 at Ewood—the season that Blackburn won the FA Cup.

It was an unusual match in many ways. Before it began two hymns were played by the band in memory of Bob Marshall, the Rovers player who had died that week, following an accidental injury in a Central League match at Blackpool. Gibson and Jack scored in the first half to put Wanderers 2–0 up, but the home side had lost both full-backs, Hutton and Jones, through injury. In the second half both returned, Jones at outside-left and Hutton in goal as Rovers' goalkeeper Cope hurt his shoulder in making a save. Joe Smith scored two further goals for the visitors and then Jack scored from a twice-taken penalty. In the

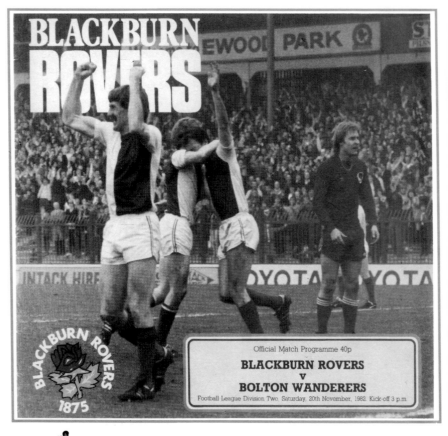

Official Match Programme 40p

BLACKBURN ROVERS
v
BOLTON WANDERERS
Football League Division Two. Saturday, 20th November, 1982. Kick-off 3 p.m.

The programme cover for a Rovers v. Bolton Wanderers derby match, in November 1982. On this occasion the score was 1–1, with Kevin Stonehouse scoring from a penalty. As ever, the choice of photograph for the programme cover was completely unpartisan!

closing minutes Butler got Bolton's sixth goal with Mitchell netting a consolation for Rovers.

One of the best-remembered clashes between Rovers and Wanderers is the FA Cup semi-final of 1957–8 at Maine Road. For twenty minutes or so, Blackburn looked well set for Wembley and Peter Dobing put the Rovers in the lead, but defensive slips allowed Ralph Gubbins to score twice in a matter of minutes.

There was another occasion when the Wanderers beat the Rovers in the Cup and went on to lift the trophy; in fact, they took it from Blackburn. In 1929 they beat Rovers in a Burnden replay after the first meeting had set up an Ewood attendance record of 61,783.

Of importance to both sides, if for different reasons, was the Second Division clash at Burnden Park on 23 March 1976, when Rovers were fighting for survival and Wanderers had high hopes of promotion. In the event, the only goal of the game, scored by John Waddington, helped save Rovers from relegation, while it was to prove a fatal blow to Bolton's hopes of returning to the top flight.

Bolton gained some consolation on 27 April 1978 when their 1–0 win at Ewood, with Frank Worthington getting the goal, ensured their promotion to the First Division. Whilst mentioning the First Division, the season 1963–4 was a truly memorable one for the Rovers, who completed the 'double' against their near neighbours. It was 3–0 at Ewood and 5–0 at Burnden. Another notable result was Rovers' 5–0 win at Burnden on 29 March 1963 when John Byrom—later to join Bolton—scored two of the goals.

Boundary Park

ON BOXING DAY 1981 Oldham Athletic were beaten 3–0 at home by Blackburn Rovers. The match had been switched from Blackburn by mutual agreement because Oldham's Boundary Park pitch was playable, unlike Ewood. The Football League at first ruled that the match would still count as a home fixture for Blackburn, but altered their decision to record it as a home game for Oldham. Rovers' scorers were Garner, Stonehouse and Bell, in what was Oldham's first home defeat that season.

Bradford Park Avenue

PARK AVENUE enjoyed forty-seven seasons in the league before failing to hold on to their place in 1969–70 after three consecutive seasons at the bottom of the league.

They started their career in the Second Division in 1908–9 and in 1914 joined their Bradford neighbours, City, in the First Division. The clubs first met on the opening day of the 1914–15 season, Rovers winning at Bradford 2–1.

They were relegated in 1920–1 and the following season suffered the embarrassment of dropping into the Third Division (North). They returned to the Second Division in 1928 and it was not until 1950–1 that they were next relegated. In 1937–8 Rovers were beaten 7–1 at Park Avenue, though the following season saw them gain revenge by completing the 'double' for the only time—6–4 at Ewood and 4–0 at Park Avenue.

Founder members of the Fourth Division, Bradford won promotion just once more before their eventual demise.

Tommy Briggs

TOMMY BRIGGS was a centre-forward in the traditional mould: a man who relied upon others to create chances which he converted with great consistency. Though he was not the most skilful of players, the power of his heading, running and shooting made him a feared opponent.

Born in Chesterfield on 27 November 1923, Tommy Briggs was a butcher by trade and played junior football in the Doncaster area. During the war years he served in the Royal Navy and, being stationed in Plymouth, he was a guest player for Argyle. In May 1947 he arrived on trial at Grimsby Town and over the next four seasons he scored eighty-seven goals in 135 appearances. In 1949–50 he not only topped Grimsby's scoring charts but was also the top marksman in the Football League with 36 goals, and in January of that year was capped by the England 'B' team.

Moving to Coventry City for £20,000, he scored seven goals in eleven appearances, but was unable to settle and joined Birmingham City. After a good first season at St Andrews he was allowed to move to Rovers for £15,000.

Tommy Briggs was hugely popular with the Ewood faithful and in each of four successive seasons topped thirty league goals. In 1954–5 he was again the league's leading scorer with thirty-three goals, including seven in succession in the 8–3 win over Bristol Rovers.

The 1957–8 season brought an end to his Ewood career when he lost form and doubts were raised about his fitness. He was allowed to return to Grimsby and later moved to Glentoran as player-manager.

Although Simon Garner broke Tommy Briggs' league aggregate scoring record in terms of goals per game, Briggs remains the most prolific league scorer in the club's modern history.

Jack Bruton

A FORMER PIT LAD, Jack Bruton began his player career with Horwich RMI and then had trials with Bolton Wanderers. However, it was at Turf Moor where he established himself as one of the best wingers in the country—it was reported that he came up from the pit and signed professional forms on an overturned tub at the pit head.

While with Burnley he won representative honours with the Football League team and made three appearances for England.

When he moved to Blackburn in December 1929 for £6,500, it was the most that the Ewood Park club had ever paid for a player. A maker of goals as well as a scorer, Bruton proved to be remarkably consistent during his playing career with Rovers.

On retiring from playing, Bruton remained at Ewood as an assistant trainer and assistant secretary. During manager Will Scott's enforced absence, Bruton took over the running of the club and on Scott's return was appointed assistant manager. He was the natural successor when Rovers' lack of consistency led to Scott finally vacating the manager's chair.

On taking control his immediate aim was to avoid the team's relegation, but nine defeats in the last ten games sealed the club's fate.

Bruton quickly took steps in an attempt to bounce straight back. Dennis Westcott, a proven goal-scorer from Wolves, was signed, whilst Bruton unearthed an exciting prospect at left-back in the shape of Bill Eckersley. However, success proved just as elusive and after the club finished in fourteenth place in the Second Division, Bruton was summoned to a board meeting and released.

Jack Bruton refused to accept total responsibility for Rovers' plight, claiming that he always had to submit his team selection to the board who, if they so wished, altered it, and that he did not have full control in the buying and selling of players. In a parting statement he said, 'My earnest wish is that the next manager will receive more co-operation.' With that, Jack Bruton ended a twenty-year association with Blackburn Rovers.

Burial

BLACKBURN ROVERS would probably have preferred to pass quietly and anonymously into the Second and Third Divisions when they were relegated, but the people of Bamber Bridge, near Preston, did not give them the choice. Mock burials of football teams are a long-established tradition in Bamber Bridge. The idea first started among regulars of the White Bull, who brought funeral flowers whenever one of their teams was relegated. Since then it has developed into a full-scale funeral procession—bands, floats, hundred-year-old hearses, pall bearers, black-clad mourners—the whole works. When a

> *In Remembrance of*
> *Blackburn Rovers*
> *Who Passed Peacefully and Effortlessly*
> *Into the Third Division 1970-71*
>
> As this soul passes on
> Shed no tears of grief
> For as the end came in sight
> Resistance was so brief
>
> *R.I.P.*   *After long and intense Suffering*

team is promoted, a 'resurrection' procession, complete with Morris dancers and brass bands, marches through the streets of Bamber Bridge.

Burnley

THE RIVALRY between Blackburn Rovers and Burnley stretches right back to the early days of the Football League. During the 1889–90 season, Rovers visited Turf Moor in a league game and, despite an early Burnley goal, triumphed 2–1. Burnley's Claude Lambie had a goal disallowed by the referee who, it turned out, was the brother of Blackburn's goalkeeper John Horne! Not surprisingly, Burnley complained, but Rovers got in ahead of them, complaining about the intimidation of the Burnley crowd. The Rovers also made a similar complaint a couple of months later when Burnley beat them in the Lancashire Cup final.

Burnley are also the only team that Rovers have ever beaten 7–1 at home and away in the First Division!

There have been a number of memorable clashes between the two clubs over the years, but perhaps none have matched the fireworks provided by both teams in a First Division match at Ewood Park on 9 November 1929. The poor weather and two under-strength teams kept many supporters at home. Those that did brave the elements had little to cheer about in the opening stages as Burnley pressed forward. Then after twenty-five minutes Groves scored for Rovers from Imrie's cross. Burnley equalised from a controversial penalty before Roscamp re-stored Rovers' lead just on half-time. Burnley started the second half with Devine on the field but not fully fit, and Rovers made the most of the situation as Roscamp, McLean and Imrie all scored. The Clarets, to their credit, refused to accept defeat and pulled a goal back through an own-goal by Page after fine approach work by Bruton. Within minutes, though, McLean and Groves added further goals for Rovers before McCluggage netted his second penalty of the match for the visitors. In the last minute Groves scored his third goal to give Rovers a convincing 8–3 victory over their old rivals.

In 1959–60, when Burnley won the League Championship, the two teams met at Turf Moor in the sixth round of the FA Cup. Although goal-less at half-time, the Clarets scored three goals within a fifteen-minute period early in the second half. However, following a fortuitous penalty awarded against Elder, Douglas put the spot-kick away to bring Rovers back in the game. Three minutes later Peter Dobing hit a terrific twenty-five-yard drive past an unsighted Blacklaw. Time appeared to be running out for Rovers but, with just four minutes remaining, McGrath sent the Blackburn contingent in the 51,501 crowd wild as his sliced shot entered the net.

The replay at Ewood produced another full house. Rovers totally outplayed Burnley to win 2–0 and went all the way to Wembley.

By Gum!

BLACKBURN ROVERS joined the ever-increasing band of clubs who recorded their own songs in 1973. Entitled 'By Gum We'll Make it a Day', the 'B' side was a specially recorded song by a group of fans, 'Come On the Rovers'. Rehearsals for the record were held in Ewood Working Men's Club, just across the road from the ground. Needless to say, the record didn't make the top twenty!

Canaries

WHEN BLACKBURN ROVERS entertained Birmingham City on 21 February 1935 in the fifth round of the FA Cup, the youngest spectator was a canary with blue and white plumage. As the official club's mascot, its job was to chirp the Rovers to victory.

Blue and white canaries were uncommon; there were only odd ones in Blackburn. But that was not the only reason for the sudden rise to fame for this canary—known as Cock o'the North—for his grandfather was once a Rovers' mascot and went with them to Wembley when they won the cup in 1928. The grandson's feathers were the colour of the

Rovers' shirts; the cage, too, was blue and white. It was enclosed in a box painted in blue and white quarters and bore the messages 'Chirps from Blackburn', 'Play Up Rovers!' and 'Cock o'the North—Rovers' Mascot'. On top of the cage was a card outlining his future—'To Wembley via Birmingham'.

Unfortunately, he didn't sing loud enough, for Rovers lost 1–2.

Captains

ONE OF THE CLUB's earliest captains was Jimmy Brown, a solicitor's clerk by profession. He became a firm favourite with the Blackburn public and, in an era when physical strength often dominated, Brown's delicate touch and devastating pace were capable of destroying the best of defences. He captained the Rovers to their three FA Cup triumphs in the 1880s and was capped five times for England. After the third FA Cup victory Brown finally bowed out of football, but was brought back briefly during the club's first season in the Football League.

As a captain, Bob Crompton ensured that all the Rovers team followed his own high standards of fair play, for he played the game in the true Corinthian spirit. He had natural leadership qualities for

Jimmy Brown, one of the Club's earliest captains.

captaincy and yet was never 'one of the boys'. He was club captain of two championship-winning sides and also captain of England.

The ability of Harry Healless to organise his playing colleagues, coupled with his tough tackling and sound headwork, made him a natural choice for the captaincy. Capped twice for England, his proudest moment came when he held the FA Cup aloft in 1928 after leading the side to victory over Huddersfield Town.

Walter Crook was not given an extended run in the Rovers side until the 1934–5 season and from 22 December 1934 until the outbreak of war he remained an ever-present. A hard, physical player whose aggressive approach inspired those around him, he led the team to the Second Division Championship in 1938–9.

One of Blackburn-s all-time greats, Ronnie Clayton was a tremendous driving force in the club's promotion back to the First Division in 1957–8. A brilliant defender, Clayton also liked to power forward and instigate attacking moves. His natural leadership qualities showed early in his career and, as well as captaining Rovers, he led England for the last five of his thirty-five appearances.

Glenn Keeley became captain following his return from a loan spell at Everton and led the club to their first Wembley triumph since 1928 when he captained the side in the 1987 Full Members' Cup final.

In recent years, and after giving outstanding service to Manchester City, Nicky Reid captained Rovers to the play-offs in his first three seasons with the club.

Johnny Carey

ARRIVING AT OLD TRAFFORD in 1936, Johnny Carey embarked on what was to be a highly successful playing career with Manchester United. A versatile and gifted performer, he was capped by both the Republic of Ireland and Northern Ireland, was Footballer of the Year in 1949 and helped United win the League Championship in 1951–2.

Joining Rovers as manager in 1953, Carey was keen to pursue and improve Rovers' existing youth policy, but also realised that the team needed a touch of experience. As a result, Bobby Langton, the old

Johnny Carey: His attacking brand of football produced goals galore and the crowds flocked to Ewood Park after the joined the Club as Manager in 1953 after a successful playing career with Manchester United.

Rovers' winger, was brought back to the club where he first made his name.

For four consecutive seasons, Carey took Rovers to the brink of the First Division with an attacking brand of football that produced goals galore. The crowds flocked to Ewood Park as the quiet, pipe-smoking Irishman introduced the youngsters who would form the team known as Carey's Chicks. Peter Dobing and Roy Vernon lined up alongside Clayton, Douglas and McGrath, whilst Harry Leyland and Matt Woods were brought from Everton to strengthen the defence. The side was complete when Ally MacLeod arrived from St Mirren and, in 1957–8, promotion was finally achieved.

Unfortunately for Rovers, Carey's achievements had not gone unnoticed, and in October 1958 he left Ewood to manage Everton. His stay on Merseyside was a short one, however, and his dismissal at the end of the 1960–1 season was bizarre, to say the least. He was sacked while sharing a taxi with his club chairman! He then took over the reins

at Leyton Orient and later enjoyed a successful spell with Nottingham Forest from 1963 to 1968.

In January 1969 Carey accepted Blackburn's invitation to take care of administration matters, whilst Eddie Quigley continued to take charge of the playing affairs. However, in October 1970 the board decided that the two should swap positions and so Carey took charge of the team for a second time.

Despite a brief revival early in 1971, the club was relegated to the Third Division for the first time in its history. The jovial Irishman, along with Quigley, paid the price which relegation usually brings. Johnny Carey had been unable to work his magic for a second time.

Jack Carr

As a PLAYER with Newcastle United, his only club, Jack Carr had won two England caps, three League Championship medals, an FA Cup-winner's medal and two runners-up medals. On hanging up his boots, he became assistant trainer at St James' Park and remained there until he became Blackburn's first full-time manager in February 1922.

At Blackburn he faced a monumental task as the club struggled in the years immediately following the war; and though Rovers had the resources to to bring in new men, success continued to elude the manager. In fact, during his reign Rovers' highest position was eighth—hardly the level of success the Blackburn board were hoping for. Carr also suffered some embarrassing defeats in the FA Cup, notably at the hands of Corinthians and South Shields.

The club's first flirtation with professional management was brought to an end in December 1926 when Jack Carr resigned his position. It has to be said that the experiment had not been a success, and the Rovers board were in no rush to repeat the exercise.

Centuries

Goals: BLACKBURN ROVERS have scored a century of goals in a Football League season on one occasion. The club scored 114 goals in 1954–5 to finish sixth in the Second Division.

There are nine instances of individual players who have scored a hundred or more goals for the Rovers. Simon Garner is the greatest goal-scorer with 186 strikes in his Blackburn career (1978–92), while Tommy Briggs scored 143 goals between 1952 and 1957. Other century-scorers are Ted Harper and Jack Southworth, both of whom scored 122 goals for the Rovers, Jack Bruton (115), Bryan Douglas (111), Eddie Latheron (104), Peter Dobing (104) and Andy McEvoy (103).

Appearances: ONLY Reg Elvy has made over a hundred consecutive appearances immediately after making his Football League debut.

Chairmen

BELOW IS A full list of the Rovers chairmen.

J. Lewis	1875–88	G. N. Forbes	1956–60
E. S. Morley	1888–1901	J. Wilkinson	1960–4
R. Birtwistle	1901–5	D. Hull	1964–8
L. Cotton	1905–18	C. R. Davies	1968–70
C. Cotton	1918–21	A. L. Fryars	1970–1
J. W. Walsh	1921–33	W. H. Bancroft	1971–9
W. Tempest	1933–8	D. T. Keighley	1979
J. Cotton	1938–43	D. Brown	1979–82
J. Caton	1944–8	W. Fox	1982–91
F. Wood	1948–52	R. D. Coar	1991–
T. Blackshaw	1952–6		

Championships

BLACKBURN ROVERS have on four occasions won a divisional championship.

1911–12 First Division Champions

The rebuilding programme which the directors embarked upon finally paid dividends as the Rovers landed their first League Championship. Having added Jock Simpson to the team during the latter part of the 1910–11 season, the club lost only one of seventeen games in the middle of the season.

	P	W	D	L	F	A	Pts
Blackburn Rovers	38	20	9	9	60	43	49
Everton	38	20	6	12	46	42	46
Newcastle United	38	18	8	12	64	50	44

The Blackburn Rovers side that won the First Division Championship in 1911–12 and 1913–14.

1913–14 First Division Champions

The Rovers got off to a fine start, winning their opening five games and remaining undefeated in the first ten. This was to set the pattern as Simpson, Shea (signed from West Ham United), Latheron and Hodkinson began to blend together. Losing only seven games all season—a club record—the team was superbly organised on the field by the ever-reliable Crompton.

	P	W	D	L	F	A	Pts
Blackburn Rovers	38	20	11	7	78	42	51
Aston Villa	38	19	6	13	65	50	44
Oldham Athletic	38	17	9	12	55	45	43

1938–9 Second Division Champions

The season was one of triumphant progress, for the Rovers were never lower than sixth in the table. They went to the top just before Christmas and for the last twenty-three weeks of the season, except for one Saturday when they dropped to second place, they remained in the leading position.

	P	W	D	L	F	A	Pts
Blackburn Rovers	42	25	5	12	94	60	55
Sheffield United	42	20	14	8	69	41	54
Sheffield Wednesday	42	21	11	10	88	59	53

1974–5 Third Division Champions

Arriving at Ewood Park in January 1974, manager Gordon Lee quietly set about rebuilding the Rovers team. His new-look side stormed to the top of the Third Division and remained there for most of the season. The crowd for the final game of the season at home to Wrexham was 21,290. The result a 0–0 draw—the title belonging to Rovers.

	P	W	D	L	F	A	Pts
Blackburn Rovers	46	22	16	8	68	45	60
Plymouth Argyle	46	24	11	11	79	58	59
Charlton Athletic	46	22	11	13	76	61	55

Charity Shield

BLACKBURN ROVERS have appeared in two Charity Shield matches, the first being when they played Queen's Park Rangers at White Hart Lane. In the ordinary way of things, that match would have been played at the beginning of the 1912–13 season, but around that time the *Titanic* disaster took place, and the match was brought forward to 4 May 1912 so that the proceeds could be devoted to the Titanic Relief Fund.

Rovers won 2–1 with Wattie Aitkenhead scoring both goals after Revill had scored for Rangers.

In their second Charity Shield appearance on 28 October 1928, Rovers played Everton at Old Trafford, but lost 1–2.

Ronnie Clayton

BORN IN PRESTON on 8 August 1934, Ronnie Clayton joined the Rovers in 1949, making his league debut at the age of sixteen in the 1950–1 season. His early promise led the Blackburn manager, then Jackie Bestall, to predict an England future for the talented youngster. Clayton had natural leadership qualities which showed early in his career. In September 1955 he won his first Under-23 cap and a month later he appeared for the England 'B' team. In November of that year he completed the international sequence when he made his debut for the full England team.

He was a tremendous driving force in Blackburn's promotion back to the First Division in 1957–8. Clayton was an energetic wing-half,

 Ronnie Clayton: One of Blackburn Rovers' all-time greats.

strong in the tackle and brilliant timer of the ball in the air. He also liked to power forward and instigate attacking moves.

He provided Ewood supporters with many magic moments during his long career, but there are perhaps few to rival the moment he scored a vital equalising goal in an FA Cup tie against Liverpool. It was during Rovers' promotion season of 1957–8 where they had already seen off Rotherham, Everton and Cardiff. There was a full house at Ewood Park to see a tense cup-tie in which Liverpool went in at half-time one up. There were just ten minutes left when Clayton, Rovers' courageous captain, came back to the field after touchline treatment.

He was just in time to line up for a free kick awarded against Liverpool. Roy Vernon took it out on the right wing and lobbed it towards the far post, where Clayton, moving more quickly than anyone else, flung himself forward to connect with his forehead and send the ball into the corner of the net. It completely changed the course of the game for, a minute later, Ally MacLeod grabbed the winner. It wasn't until the following Monday that it was discovered that Clayton had in fact chipped his kneecap!

He appeared in the final stages of the 1958 World Cup in Sweden and succeeded Billy Wright as captain for the last five of his thirty-five England appearances. He then lost favour with the England selectors and, surprisingly, didn't play again for his country after 1960.

He continued to give good service to Blackburn and led them to Wembley in 1960, only for them to lose 0–3 to Wolverhampton Wanderers. Remaining loyal to what many would class an unfashionable club, Ronnie Clayton experienced the highs and lows, but always maintained the same level of enthusiasm and endeavour. As age began to slow down his legs, he moved to play at the heart of the defence, where he became a very accomplished centre-back. It was Clayton's masterful reading of the game that provided the solid defensive platform for the team.

At the end of the 1968–9 season he finally left Ewood Park to become player-manager at Morecambe. He returned to Ewood once more in December 1970 for a well-deserved testimonial before returning to north-east Lancashire to team up with Great Harwood.

Throughout a career that spanned nineteen seasons, Ronnie Clayton remained one of football's finest ambassadors. He was, without doubt, one of the greatest players ever to wear the Rovers' colours.

Clean Sheet

THIS IS THE colloquial expression to describe a goalkeeper's performance when he does not concede a goal.

In the Football league, Jim Arnold kept nineteen clean sheets in thirty-eight appearances when Rovers won the Third Division Championship in 1979–80, whilst Reg Elvy kept eighteen clean sheets from a full forty-two-match programme in 1953–4, though he did concede eight goals at Lincoln City!

Colours

WITH AN EARLY influence from the public schools, the Rovers' kit is adapted from the colours of Malvern School, with Cambridge blue taking the place of Malvern green on the instantly-recognisable halved shirts. The Rovers have always had blue and white quarters, though there was one brief period when for a short time they had blue and white 'eighths'.

The present shirts, like the original ones, are blue down one side at the front and white down the other side, with two halves reversed at the back, so that if the shirt were opened out there would be two quarters of blue and two quarters of white. The shirts worn for a short time had four quarterings on the front and four on the back.

However, when Blackburn played Sheffield Wednesday in the 1890 FA Cup final at Kennington Oval, they played in white evening dress shirts with full fronts and a stud in the centre to avoid clashing with the blue and white stripes of the Owls.

In those days, clubs could play in any colours they wished. There was one match on the Leamington Street ground when Preston North End, in an effort to bewilder the Rovers in a 'blood match', actually played in seven different colours!

For the FA Cup final with Huddersfield Town in 1928, the Rovers wore dark blue jerseys and white shorts, and Huddersfield white

jerseys and blue shorts. The Rovers did not use those jerseys again after that final.

Consecutive Home Games

THE ROVERS have been involved in two intense sequences of six home games in succession, being unbeaten in both of them. In 1892–3 they won four and drew two of that sequence, but in 1927–8 they won all six games. After playing away at Birmingham City on 4 February 1927 and losing 1–2, Rovers were involved in the following list of matches at Ewood Park, before visiting Huddersfield Town on 14 March, where they lost 1–3.

Date	Opponents	Competition	Score
11 February	Newcastle United	Division One	1–0
18 February	Port Vale	FA Cup Round 5	2–1
23 February	Middlesbrough	Division One	3–0
25 February	Tottenham Hotspur	Division One	2–1
3 March	Manchester United	FA Cup Round 6	2–0
10 March	Liverpool	Division One	2–1

Cricketers

THE ROVERS have had five players who were also cricketers of real distinction. The first of these was A. N. 'Monkey' Hornby. He was captain of Lancashire County Cricket Club for fourteen seasons and is still rated as one of the greatest opening batsmen of all time. He scored 10,649 runs for the county and played in three Tests. His connection with Blackburn lay in the fact that his family owned cotton mills in the town. An all-round sportsman, he played international rugby and was well known for his performances in games of Harrow-rules football played at that time.

A. N. 'Monkey' Hornby: Rovers' first cricketer of real distinction.

Hugh McIntyre enjoyed great success with Blackburn, winning three winners' medals in his four FA Cup final appearances. His all-round sporting ability led to his representing Lancashire as wicket-keeper for one match in 1884.

Arthur Paul was a goalkeeper and another Lancashire County cricketer. It was he who partnered Archie MacLaren in a record-breaking fourth-wicket stand against Somerset at Taunton in 1895, when MacLaren went on to make 424—Paul's share was 177. His only game for the Rovers came at the Hawthorns in 1889–90 when West Bromwich won 3–2.

So good a soccer player was Joe Hulme, an England international, that as a cricketer he has been underestimated. But he was a very able batsman who, for a period, was second only to Patsy Hendren in the Middlesex side. Signed from York City for a small fee, his great assets of searing pace and fine centring soon had the big clubs after him, and Arsenal paid £1,500 to take him to Highbury and national fame.

The most recent county cricketer to wear the colours of Blackburn Rovers is Henry Horton. He came to Ewood from Worcester City, creating a little bit of soccer history because the fee of £2,000 was a record paid for a non-league player. Tall and straight-backed, Horton was a sterling utility half-back or forward for several seasons before his transfer to Southampton in 1951–2. As a cricketer, he began his career at New Road, Worcester, but was unable to gain a regular place. Moving to Hampshire, he scored 21,536 runs for the southern county before his retirement from the first-class game in 1967.

 Bob Crompton: The greatest 'Rover' of them all.

Bob Crompton

AN APPRENTICE PLUMBER, Bob Crompton was also a keen swimmer and water polo player, who arrived at Blackburn Rovers in September 1896. However, he delayed signing professional forms for two years as he did not want to jeopardise his amateur status and, also, he had nearly finished his apprenticeship as a plumber.

His plumbing provided him with an independent income, for on completion of his apprenticeship he became a partner in the firm and patented several important inventions in the plumbing trade. Throughout his life rumours persisted that these inventions had made him a wealthy man and, though he always claimed the stories were grossly exaggerated, he did own a car at a time when few in society did!

Bob Crompton made his debut for Rovers on 10 April 1897 at Stoke City as a seventeen-year-old centre-half and remains the youngest player ever to play in that position for the club.

He won most of the honours which the game had to offer. He was club captain of two championship-winning sides, an international for over ten years, and captain of England. He had natural leadership qualities and, as captain, ensured that all the Rovers team followed his own high standards of fair play. A private man, he remained aloof from his playing colleagues, but had the authority to command respect. A talented player, he was strong in the air and could pass the ball with great accuracy for a man of his size, and the strength of his kicking was legendary. Though he made a couple of appearances in 1919–20, the First World War effectively ended his playing career. However, the end of this led a new and successful career, first as a director and then manager.

Crompton was a popular choice with the Blackburn supporters, who still regarded him as the greatest player that the club had produced. Victory against Huddersfield Town in the FA Cup final of 1928 was an unexpected boost and added to the legend of Bob Crompton. Unfortunately, while results on the field were encouraging, Bob Crompton's autocratic style of management began to cause unrest among the playing staff. As a manager he had his own beliefs on how the game should be played and, though he was prepared to listen to others, he was not prepared to compromise. Matters came to a head in

February 1931 when it was announced that the chairman had received a letter from the players pointing out alleged grievances they had against Crompton. While still a director, Crompton immediately withdrew from managerial duties until the issue was settled. In March 1931 the club held its annual meeting. Although surprising, no mention was made of the managerial dispute. However, when the votes were cast, Bob Crompton failed to gain re-election to the board, thus severing a thirty-four year association with the club.

In Crompton's absence, Rovers were relegated to the Second Division for the first time in their history. The local press who had criticised Crompton's departure now campaigned for his return. In March 1938, with the club struggling near the foot of the Second Division, the board approached Crompton. He took over on 2 April 1938, and under his guidance Blackburn managed to avoid relegation.

Hailed as a saviour, he was officially appointed the club's new manager in May 1938. He began to build a team to restore the club's flagging fortunes, and in the spring of 1939 Rovers were celebrating their return to the First Division as Second Division champions.

Ironically, it was the outbreak of war which had virtually ended his playing days; now it prevented him from establishing the club as a major force in the First Division. He took Rovers to the 1940 War Cup final, but in March 1941 he collapsed and died. The club had lost the greatest figure in its history, and so the last link with the club's great and glorious past was broken.

Crowd Trouble

HOWEVER UNWELCOME, crowd disturbances are far from a modern phenomenon at major football matches. Behaviour at Ewood Park has usually been of a high standard, and though Rovers' supporters are well-renowned for voicing their opinions at suspect referees, the occasions when their demonstrations boil over beyond the verbal are very rare indeed.

However, one such occasion did take place on Christmas Day 1890—the Rovers' first season at Ewood. The following day the Rovers were to play Wolverhampton Wanderers, and whether they were resting some of their men or whether they were treating their opponents, Darwen, as easy meat is not clear, but when the Rovers team came onto the field of play, only three or four of them were first-team players. As the prices had been increased for that day, the spectators were very annoyed.

Then the Darwen team appeared and the crowd urged them to go off, and so the Darwen captain led them off. A few minutes later the Darwen Second Eleven, who must have had free tickets to watch, came out to play; but the crowd were not going to be put off like that. Everyone got very excited and the spectators encroached on the field, pulling up the goalposts and threatening to wreck the press box. Even in those days people blamed the press when things went wrong. They tore the carpet from the reserved seats and cut it to shreds.

In the end the police quietened them and they were persuaded to leave the field by being given free tickets for another match.

On 27 November 1926 Blackburn entertained Manchester United. Immediately the final whistle was blown, Puddefoot was observed lying on the ground and the crowd, believing he had been hit by a United player after the whistle was blown, swarmed onto the field.

More followed, and eventually the United players were surrounded by hundreds of Rovers' supporters. All available police were directed to give protection to the players and it was some minutes before the latter could get clear. Hundreds of spectators hung about, and many efforts were made to get at the United players as they approached the passage to the stand. The United officials took the precaution of locking the dressing-room door and the police quickly dispersed the crowd.

Kenny Dalglish

KENNY DALGLISH took over as Blackburn's manager in October 1991 and capped his first season in charge by leading the club back to the top division in English football for the first time since 1966. He was persuaded to return to management after an eight-month holiday. He had resigned as Liverpool's manager in February 1991 through sheer exhaustion, saying he needed a break from football.

At the time he was by far the country's most outstanding manager, having led Liverpool to three League Championships. He took them to three FA Cup finals, winning two of them. His side was beaten in one League Cup final and they won the Super Cup, a competition introduced following the English ban from European football.

As a player, Dalglish won a record number of 102 caps for Scotland, and shares his country's scoring record with Denis Law, both having scored thirty goals. Brought up in the shadow of Ibrox Park, it was always assumed that Kenny Dalglish would play in the blue of Rangers, but it was Celtic who signed him.

His skills were subtle and stemmed from the balance and speed with which he controlled the ball. His passing was immaculate and his deceptive swirls in full flight would often send defenders the wrong way. In six seasons as a Celtic regular, he was on three occasions their leading goal-scorer. He hit 166 league and cup goals, won five league titles, four Scottish Cups and a Scottish League Cup-winners' medal.

Dalglish was already a legend when he joined Liverpool for £440,000 in 1977. At the time it was a record fee for an English club. He ended his first season as top scorer as Liverpool stormed to the league title again and Dalglish was voted Footballer of the Year. He was instrumental in Liverpool's winning the 1978 European Cup final against Bruges, scoring the only goal of the game. Liverpool continued to dominate British football and Dalglish was a key figure. In 1983 he scored his hundredth goal for Liverpool to become only the third player ever to score a century of goals in both Scottish and English football. He was also voted Footballer of the Year again and picked up the Player of the Year award as the Reds won their fourteenth championship.

During his career Kenny Dalglish bagged a total of 367 goals in club and international football—a marvellous achievement.

On taking over at Ewood he immediately proceeded to rebuild the side. They looked set for one of the two guaranteed promotion places, but blew their chances when losing six games in succession at a critical time. But they recovered to qualify for the play-offs and, after beating Derby County 5–4 on aggregate in the semi-final, they went on to defeat Leicester 1–0 in the Wembley final.

Darwen

RELATIONSHIPS with neighbouring Darwen were never good and many of the encounters between the two clubs were to provide some of the most hostile matches in the Rovers' history, especially in their pre-league days.

Hugh McIntyre, in only his second game for the Rovers, angered the Darwen spectators by his actions in the game at Darwen on 12 April 1879, when a long throw endangered the Rovers' goal. Without ceremony he kicked for touch with such great length that a lot of time elapsed before the ball was located in a neighbouring field.

In November 1879 Darwen's goalkeeper Duxbury fisted the ball clear. His feet had barely returned to the floor when McIntyre hit him with such force that it took several minutes, and the ministerings of Darwen's centre-forward Dr Gledhill, to restore him to consciousness.

In 1880 Fergie Suter, who was probably the first professional with Blackburn Rovers, moved from Darwen for what were termed 'personal reasons'. Suter had joined Darwen from Rangers, and although Darwen officials claimed that he was not being paid, few ever witnessed Suter carrying out his stonemasonry trade.

Ferfie Suter: probably the first professional with Blackburn Rovers.

On 27 November 1880, 10,000 witnessed a match against Darwen which saw Fergie Suter in direct opposition to his old club. A rugged encounter ended with Suter and Darwen's Marshall becoming embroiled in a fight. A good number of the crowd decided to join in and the match was abandoned. The Rovers, who were appalled by the mayhem, cancelled a return game scheduled for later in the season, and so widened the rift which already existed between the clubs.

Unfortunately, fate paired the two teams in the English Cup. After much wrangling over where and when the game should take place, it was played on 31 January 1882 at Blackburn. There was a complete transformation in supremacy since the clubs had last met, Rovers winning 5–1.

Deaths

ON BOXING DAY 1927, Bob Marshall, the club's young reserve fullback, sustained an injury in the Central League game at Blackpool which resulted in his becoming the first fatality in the club's history. He was assisted from the field, but recovered sufficiently to return to his fiancée's home in Lytham Road, where he was staying. During the night he became ill with violent pains in the abdomen and, despite an emergency operation when he was rushed to hospital, he died on 3 January 1928.

Prior to this, the club received a bitter blow when, in July 1906, Sam McClure, still at the peak of his career, died. He was taken ill at his home in Workington with an abcess behind his ear, which spread inward to the brain. Although he was rushed to the infirmary, he died before an operation could be performed.

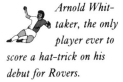

Arnold Whittaker, the only player ever to score a hat-trick on his debut for Rovers.

Debuts

THE ONLY PLAYER to score a hat-trick on his debut for the club was Arnold Whittaker, who scored all three goals in the 3–0 home victory over Preston North End on 14 October 1899.

A number of players have scored two goals on their debut for the club, the most recent being Alan Ainscow on 1 February 1986 in the home match against Hull City. Losing 2–0 to a decisively average Yorkshire side, the mercurial mid-field veteran struck twice to draw the scores level and excite the Blackburn end faithful into raptures.

A debut with a difference was that of Keith Fear who, in 1977–8, had just arrived on loan in time to play and was thrust straight into the Boxing Day clash with Burnley. During the course of the game he was asked to take a penalty, which Stevenson, the Burnley 'keeper, saved. However, Fear did have the last laugh, as he scored in a 3–2 win for Rovers.

Defeats

Individual games

BLACKBURN'S worst *home* defeat in a first-class match was the 1–7 scoreline inflicted on the club by both Notts County (14 March 1891) and Middlesbrough (29 November 1947). *Away* from home, the club's heaviest defeat has been 0–8 which has been inflicted on two occasions: *v* Arsenal (25 February 1933) and *v* Lincoln City (29 August 1953).

Over a single season

ROVERS' worst defensive record in terms of defeats suffered in a single season was in 1965–6 when the club lost thirty out of forty-two First Division matches. Conversely, the Rovers only lost seven matches in 1914–15, when they won the First Division Championship.

Consecutive league matches without defeat

BLACKBURN'S best run of league games without defeat is twenty-three and was established largely in the autumn of 1987 as the club amassed seventy-seven points to finish in the play-offs. The run began on 30 September 1987 with a 1–1 draw at Villa Park, and finished with a 2–2 draw at Elland Road against Leeds United on 27 February 1988.

Defensive Records

BLACKBURN ROVERS' *best* defensive record in the Football League was established in 1980–1, the club's first season in Division Two following promotion the previous season. The Rovers conceded just twenty-nine goals in that campaign and were beaten in only eight matches.

The club's *worst* defensive record in the Football League was in 1932–3 when they let in 102 goals in forty-two matches to finish fifteenth in the First Division.

Dismissals

ALTHOUGH SENDINGS-OFF are an all-too-common feature of the modern game, no-one should think that football has ever been immune from them. The first Rovers player to be sent off in a Football League match was Joe Lofthouse. He was dismissed, along with Burnley's Stewart, for fighting as Rovers went down 0–3 at Turf Moor on 12 December 1891.

The first goalkeeper to be sent off was Terry Gennoe, who was dismissed for handball on 30 October 1982 in the match against Charlton Athletic at the Valley—Rovers losing this game 3–0.

During the first Premier League season three Blackburn players were shown the red card—Tim Sherwood at Goodison Park for comments made to a linesman, and Tony Dobson and Mike Newell at Selhurst Park in the match against Wimbledon, whose Vinny Jones was also dismissed.

Bryan Douglas

BRYAN DOUGLAS' only ambition as a youngster was to wear the blue and white of Blackburn Rovers. Practically living on the doorstep of Ewood Park, he joined his home-town team as a groundstaff boy in 1952, after he had much success with Blackburn Schoolboys.

Unfortunately for Bryan and Blackburn, National Service disrupted his early career and he did not make his first-team debut until 1954. During those early days in the team he was often criticised for being over-elaborate and too selfish. Deceptively frail-looking at 5 ft. 6 ins., he was later to confound those critics and become one of England's greatest post-war footballers. He had helped Blackburn to

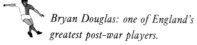
Bryan Douglas: one of England's greatest post-war players.

win promotion from Division Two in 1957–8, when they finished one point behind West Ham United. That was the season he made his England debut against Wales, wearing Stanley Matthews' number 7 shirt. Considering that Douglas played in the era of Finney, Matthews, Charlton, Haynes and Greaves, he did well to play for his country so often. In fact, he won thirty-six caps and scored eleven goals—an excellent return for a winger. Blackburn preferred to use him as a scheming inside-forward. He hit his passes beautifully and used to sit in the centre of mid-field knocking the ball around.

One of the days to be remembered in Rovers' history was the day that manager Johnny Carey switched Douglas to outside-right as Roy Vernon went away to do his National Service. The Rovers romped home against a poor Bury side at Gigg Lane 4–0, with Douglas scoring the third after cheekily walking round goalkeeper Conway.

Bryan Douglas had the most perfect close control it is possible to see. His shuffling feet carved up opposing defences for more than a decade, during which he made a succession of forwards—notably Fred Pickering and Andy McEvoy—into frequent goal-scorers with his inch-perfect passes. On a muddy Upton Park pitch in 1963–4 he was the executioner-in-chief as Pickering and McEvoy both claimed hat-tricks as Rovers beat West Ham 8–2.

Probably the two high points in Bryan's distinguished career were playing in the 1960 FA Cup final, where Rovers lost 0–3 to Wolves, and then playing in all four of England's games in the 1962 World Cup

in Chile. A cartilage operation, coupled with other injuries, meant that he missed most of Blackburn's struggle against relegation in 1965–6. The 1966–7 season was his last as a truly effective member of the Rovers' first-team squad, as his final years at Ewood were dogged by injury. He finally retired from the first-class game at the end of the 1968–9 season and spent a couple of seasons playing non-league football for Great Harwood with Ronnie Clayton and Roy Vernon.

A brilliant ball-playing forward, Bryan Douglas made up for a lack of height and physical strength with great vision and artistry.

Draws

BLACKBURN played their greatest number of drawn league matches in a single season (eighteen) in 1980–1, when they finished fourth in the Second Division after winning promotion in the previous season; and their *fewest* (two) in seasons 1890–1 and 11893–4.

The club's highest scoring draw is 5–5, a scoreline in three Rovers' matches: Accrington (home 1888–9, the club's opening game in the Football League); Arsenal (home 1962–3); and Birmingham City (away 1964–5).

The greatest number of drawn matches in a single Blackburn FA Cup tie is two. This happened in four ties: Portsmouth (1899–1900); Tottenham Hotspur (1906–7); Portsmouth (1924–5); and Sunderland (1938–9).

East Lancs Charity Cup

IIT WAS IN MAY 1882 that representatives of Blackburn Rovers, Olympic, Darwen and Accrington met at the White Bull Hotel at Blackburn and decided to get an East Lancashire Charity Cup. Rovers' results in those pre-league days were:

Date	Stage	Opponents	Venue	Score
26 May 1882	Semi-final	Darwen	Away	4–1
7 Aug. 1882	Final	Blackburn Olympic	Home	2–5

Date	Stage	Opponents	Venue	Score
7 April 1883	Semi-final	Darwen	Home	2–0
2 May 1883	Final	Blackburn Olympic	Darwen	6–3
26 April 1884	Semi-final	Accrington	Home	1–1
10 May 1884	Semi-final (replay)	Accrington	Padiham	1–2
25 April 1885	Semi-final	Accrington	Home	0–1
22 May 1886	Semi-final	Accrington	Home	2–1
27 May 1886	Final	Blackburn Olympic	Away	2–0
7 May 1887	Semi-final	Darwen	Away	3–0
21 May 1887	Final	Accrington	Away	0–1
19 May 1888	Semi-final	Blackburn Olympic	Away	5–2
9 June 1888	Final	Accrington	Home	3–3

Bill Eckersley

BILL ECKERSLEY was an ex-lorry driver from Southport who might never have played for Blackburn Rovers if they hadn't been a man short for an 'A' team fixture at Feniscowles. He got to play in borrowed boots with string for shoelaces and only a couple of studs on each boot!

What a player he was, joining the Rovers in November 1947 at a time when the club was struggling to recover from the repercussions of war. In the last game of the 1947–8 campaign the Rovers, who were already doomed to relegation, gave him a first-team chance. In the course of the next few seasons he matured into the club's outstanding player, after quickly establishing himself in the first team.

Though lacking in height and weight (he was so small he could stand under a table!), his tackling was keen and he had a tremendous amount of composure and style. He was a most constructive and attacking full-back. He had the clever knack of making a winger go the way he wanted to, and, though he was aggressive, he could be very subtle, too, when required. Bill's distribution was first class but, unlike some of today's full-backs, he made sure he did his defensive job first. He gained selection for England regularly as Alf Ramsey's partner,

 Bill Eckersley: one of the finest full-backs ever to wear the black and white of Blackburn Rovers.

winning seventeen caps between 1950 and 1953. Perhaps he should have had a lot more, for he was extremely tenacious, very fit and quick.

Despite his success on the international scene, club honours eluded him. A number of promotion near-misses and two FA Cup semi-finals were all that were achieved during his prime. Unfortunately for Bill,

his career was coming to an end when promotion was finally achieved in 1958. He was plagued by injuries and missed the 1960 FA Cup run.

As club captain he led the side by example off the field; while off it, his sharp sense of humour kept the dressing-room morale high. He was completely immune to the pressures that the game brought. When he was confronted with a last-minute penalty in an FA Cup tie against West Bromwich Albion, he not only dealt with the goalkeeper's games-manship, but topped it with a smiling retort before smashing the ball into the back of the net!

During his final two seasons he only made a handful of appearances—it was a crying shame that the knee injury came along to close his career. He retired in 1961 and a crowd of 21,000 turned up to pay him an emotional farewell at Ewood in his testimonial.

Unfortunately, his life outside the game wasn't kind to him, and a confectionary business he ran near Ewood wasn't a success. He returned to driving during his later days, before he died at the tragically early age of fifty-four. The ashes of this player of limitless talent were scattered on the Ewood turf by his sons, Billy and Stephen, in an emotional ceremony before a first-team game.

Ever-presents

THERE HAVE BEEN sixty-seven Blackburn Rovers players who have been ever-present throughout a Football League season. The greatest number of ever-present seasons by a Rovers' player is four, the record being held by Walter Crook and Derek Fazackerley. The full list is:

No. of Seasons	Players
4	W. Crook, D. Fazackerley.
3	J. Bruton, R. Jones, M. Rathbone.
2	E. Bell, R. Clayton, G. Dewar, B. Douglas, R. Elby, J. Forbes, M. McGrath, A. Ogilvie, T. Parkes, R. Suart, B. Wilson, M. Woods.

No. of Seasons	Players
1	W. Aitkenhead, J. Ashcroft, M. Atkins, S. Barker, J. Barton, C. Binns, J. Branagan, T. Brandon, L. Butt, T. Briggs, J. Campbell, G. Campbell, J. Cameron, J. Carver, H. Chippendale, A. Cowell, B. Crompton, J. Dewhurst, F. Else, B. Eckersley, M. Ferguson, S. Garner, B. Guest, T. Harper, R. Haworth, C. Hendry, K. Hird, J. Hodkinson, W. Hulse, J. Hulme, A. Hunter, W. Joyce, G. Keeley, W. Kelly, B. Langton, J. Lowey, H. Leyland, D. Martin, I. Miller, B. Mimms, F. Mooney, J. Murray, J. Patterson, N. Reid, A. Rigby, S. Sellars, J. Southworth, L. Thorpe, J. Weddle, T. Wylie.

Ewood Park

IN COMMON WITH much urban development in industrial Lancashire, Ewood Park was built in the late-Victorian period. The ground was opened in April 1882 and during the 1880s it had staged football, athletics and dog-racing, among other activities. It was 1890 when the Rovers found their new home and moved into Ewood Park. The first match there was against Accrington in September of that year, but the following Christmas brought crowd trouble. Darwen were the visitors, and so incensed were their supporters when Rovers saw fit to field only three first-team players, that they pulled up and broke the goalposts, smashed dressing-room windows and tore up carpets in the reserved seating section.

The new venue was an immediate success. In 1891 England staged an international match against Scotland at Ewood Park, whilst an early attempt at floodlit football was made in October 1892, also for a game against Darwen. Then in 1893 Rovers bought the ground for £2,500 and at the same time the club's headquarters were moved from the Bay Horse Hotel to Ewood Park.

The ground witnessed further crowd problems during Everton's visit in January 1896, when part of a stand collapsed among a 20,000

BLACKBURN ROVERS NEW GRAND STAND.
400 FEET LONG, 36 FEET WIDE, WITH OVERHANGING EAVES 15 FEET WIDE,
SEATING ACCOMMODATION 5000, STANDING ACCOMMODATION 4000 (IN FRONT).
STEELWORK BY JOHN BOOTH & SONS, BOLTON.

crowd. Having come so close to a disaster, it came as no surprise when the club decided to become a limited liability company in July 1897.

The ground received little attention during the years on either side of 1900, but in 1903 the Darwen End of the ground was covered at a cost of £1,680 and held 12,000 spectators. The following year saw even greater improvements as the Nuttall Street stand, designed by Archibald Leitch, was built at a cost of £24,000—a considerable outlay even then—and opened on New Year's Day 1907 for a match against Preston. In between two championship wins in 1912 and 1914 the club built another stand, the double-decker Riverside stand, and in 1915 reported the capacity of Ewood Park to be a massive 70,886, including 7,000 seats.

In 1928 the wooden perimeter railing was replaced by a concrete wall, the Blackburn end was terraced and the Riverside stand re-roofed for a total outlay of £1,550. A year later Ewood saw its largest crowd—61,783—for the visit of Bolton Wanderers.

In 1958 the club installed floodlights, first used on 10 November during a friendly against Werder Bremen. Two years later a successful run in the FA Cup raised the necessary finances for the erection of a concrete cantilever roof over the Blackburn end terrace.

Ewood Park had to adapt more than most grounds to the requirements of the 1975 Safety of Sports Grounds Act. Without this work it is highly likely that more damage would have been done by a fire which broke out at the Blackburn end of the Nuttall Street stand in July 1984. The club chose a novel way of restoring the damage by building into the stand's existing structure a new block of executive boxes and a glass-fronted lounge overlooking the ground. The development, which cost about £250,000, was named the John Lewis Complex in honour of the club's founder.

Following the Bradford fire in 1985 safety checks revealed structural problems in the Riverside stand. The stand was demolished and the club replaced it with a much smaller structure, seating around 700 supporters. The material for the new stand and roof for the terracing was provided by a local firm, Walkersteel.

In keeping with many other clubs, the Rovers erected a new electronic scoreboard towards the end of the 1989–90 season.

In the summer of 1989 the pitch was dug up and a revolutionary new surface with under-soil heating was laid. The new 'Techturf' surface is based on natural grass growing through Netlon meshing. Used on Hong Kong's racecourses, it is said to have many of the benefits of artificial pitches but is still natural grass.

Derek Fazackerley

BORN IN PRESTON on 5 November 1951, Derek Fazackerley joined Blackburn Rovers virtually straight from school. He graduated to the first team in 1971, his breakthrough coinciding with one of the bleakest periods in the club's history. But through it all 'Faz', as he was fondly known to all Rovers' supporters, remained unperturbed at the centre of the defence, turning in his usually reliable performances week after week.

Dominant in the air and a strong tackler, he was the cornerstone of the Blackburn defence, with his greatest asset being his consistency. It was a tribute to his performances that on the rare occasions he had a bad match, it was noticed immediately as being totally out of character. He was also extremely quick over the ground, his pace enabling him

to recover lost ground with ease. He was always at his best when playing alongside a traditional centre-half, almost as a sweeper. His game flourished when he was partnered with Glenn Keeley; an arrangement to which Howard Kendall when he took over as manager, gave his full support.

'Faz' didn't score too many goals—twenty-four in all—but one of his more important came when he scored the only goal of a tension-charged local derby against Bolton Wanderers at Burnden Park on 28 March 1973.

Derek Fazackerley was 'Mr Consistency' to many Ewood supporters, and when he passed Ronnie Clayton's all-time appearance record for Blackburn Rovers he wrote a new page in the history of the club.

In 1979 Oldham Athletic offered £60,000 for his services but, fortunately for Rovers, he opted to stay at Ewood. In 1987, when he seemed to be at the end of his playing career, he was allowed to join Chester City as player-assistant manager. A year later he joined former Rovers' boss Bob Saxton at York City before, in February 1989, he teamed up with his old friend Martin Dobson at Bury.

He left the league scene in the summer of 1989 after having played a total of 662 league games (including appearances as substitute) before, in May 1990, he was appointed player-manager of the Finnish club Kumu.

Fernonzvarosi Torra

AT THE END of the 1910–11 season the Rovers undertook a tour to Austria and Hungary to play six games in twelve days. After beating the Vienna Association 9–1, they played two more games in the country against Oldham Athletic, losing the first 0–1 but winning the second 5–2.

When they reached Hungary the whole atmosphere changed completely. Though the first game against Budapestia FC was won easily enough by 4–1, and the second against Magyar Testyakorlock RDRC 4–0, the latter side resorted to all kinds of rough tactics. However, compared to the club's last game against Fernonzvarosi Torra, they were angels!

The Hungarian side boasted victories over Sunderland and Barnsley and draws with Celtic and Oldham Athletic and only admitted to having been beaten by Manchester United.

Within the first ten minutes Rovers were 3–0 up. Five minutes later Clennel appeared to have made it four when his shot hit the underside of the bar, bouncing down over the line and then coming back into the field of play. The Hungarian referee was undecided and went to consult an English-speaking spectator. The gentleman declined to intervene, so the Hungarian referee disallowed it. Eventually, the referee awarded the local side a penalty which Rovers' goalkeeper, Robinson, saved brilliantly. The crowd yelled for the kick to be re-taken, the referee once more left the field of play followed by Bob Crompton, the Rovers' captain, and several of his team. After a long delay the referee returned, the kick being re-taken and a goal resulting. When Rovers' forward Davies went round the goalkeeper, he was just about to tap the ball into the empty net when the goalkeeper struck him in the mouth, knocking out some of his teeth. The 'keeper immediately took to his heels and left the field. The rest of the game was played with the Hungarian crowd growing steadily more menacing towards the Rovers.

At full-time they converged on the Blackburn dressing room and were only prevented from attacking the Rovers' players by police with drawn sabres. Even so, there was a good deal of jostling, stones were thrown and windows broken!

Fire

ON THURSDAY 31 March 1977 fire severely damaged 200 seats at Ewood Park. Many of the seats were in the directors' and guests' boxes. Sections of the stand roof, underboarding and timber panelling were also damaged, and if it had not been for the swift action of a mystery resident living near the Blackburn Rovers ground, who raised the alarm, the club could have been facing disaster. The twenty firemen who fought the blaze by floodlight arrived just in time to prevent the fire from spreading through the board concourse.

First Division

BLACKBURN ROVERS were in the First Division from the 1888–9 season until the end of the 1935–6 season when, with Aston Villa—also 'old originals'—they were relegated.

The first match on 15 September 1888 saw them share ten goals with Accrington. There were a number of occasions in those early years when, faced with the prospect of Second Division football, luck came to the aid of the Rovers. In 1897–8 Burnley proposed that the First Division should be increased to eighteen clubs and that Blackburn and Newcastle should take the vacancies. In 1902–3 the final relegation place was between Rovers and Grimsby. Incredibly, in their last five matches Blackburn managed to scramble clear, taking seven points from a possible ten.

The 1911–12 season saw Blackburn Rovers finally win a League Championship and, after starting the 1913–14 campaign with five

 Blackburn Rovers, 1959–60.

straight wins, Crompton steered the club to their second League Championship.

The Rovers were promoted from the Second Division to the First at the end of the 1938–9 season, but the outbreak of war delayed their return. The club only spent two seasons in the top flight, for in 1947–8 they were relegated.

Throughout the 1950s the club was always in contention for a return to the First Division, but it was 1957–8 before this goal was achieved. Challenging for promotion throughout the season, Rovers arrived at the final match needing to win at Charlton Athletic to finish in second place behind West Ham United. To add to the occasion, Charlton only needed a point to pip the Rovers for second spot. A crowd of 56,435 witnessed a classic encounter at The Valley which saw Blackburn win 4–3.

The club's first three games back in the First Division saw them score fifteen goals and concede only one, but such a record could not be maintained, and the team failed to win in their next eight outings!

The 1963–4 campaign saw the Rovers as genuine championship contenders, serving notice on the rest of the First Division with a 7–2 thrashing of Tottenham Hotspur. However, at the height of the championship battle, Fred Pickering was sold to Everton and the club finally had to settle for seventh place. A disastrous 1965–6 season saw Blackburn slide into the Second Division, their last match in the First Division being a 1–0 defeat at home to Tottenham Hotspur.

Rovers' full playing record in the First division is as follows:

P	W	D	L	F	A	Pts
2,024	755	467	802	3,379	3,441	1,977

First Match

BELOW IS A REPORT from the *Blackburn Times* dated 18 December 1875 of a game played at Church on 11 December 1875.

On Saturday afternoon a football match was played at Church between members of the Rovers club, Blackburn and the Church

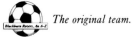 *The original team.*

club. The ball was kicked off by the Blackburn captain at three o'clock and after some fine play lasting about thirty minutes, a goal was scored by Birtwistle of the Blackburn club. With a hard struggle the Church club succeeded in scoring the next goal and the game resulted in a tie.

The original team was: Thomas Greenwood, Jack Baldwin, Fred Birtwistle, Arthur Thomas, J. T. Syckelmore, Walter Duckworth, John Lewis, Tom Dean, Arthur Constantine, Harry Greenwood and Richard Birtwistle.

First-minute Goals

PERHAPS THE ROVERS' most famous first-minute goal came in the 1928 FA Cup final against Huddersfield Town. Receiving the ball from Thornewell, Jack Roscamp found his path to goal blocked by Barkas. He produced a surprising piece of skill by chipping the ball over the startled defender, but unfortunately over-hit the ball, which floated towards Mercer in the Huddersfield goal. However, Roscamp never shirked a challenge and, as Mercer collected the ball whilst standing on the line, he dipped his right shoulder and charged into him. The ball squirmed out of the 'keeper's grip and drifted over the line.

Floodlights

ON SATURDAY 4 November 1878 Blackburn Rovers created a milestone in soccer history by becoming the first football club in the world to play a full competitive game of soccer (FA rules) under floodlights powered by electricity.

William Edwards Staite, who had invented a machine and lamps which provided power and light for large areas, and who had successfully illuminated Lime Street Station, Liverpool, approached the Rovers' committee and was given permission to erect the floodlighting for a match in which Blackburn Rovers were taking part. The occasion took place at a time when the County Palatine had dismissed electricity as a means of lighting the streets and as having no future.

The match was against Accrington at the Alexandra Meadows. A Gramme light was fixed at either end of a scaffold 30–40 ft. high, each light being attested to be of 6,000 candle-power. The attendance was nearly 6,000 and the crowd was rewarded by a fine game, Rovers winning 3–0. It was also the first occasion when a white ball was used, the leather ball being painted in order that the players could see it more clearly. In addition to the 6,000 who paid to see the game, it was estimated that a further 20,000 stood on the hills around the Meadows and enjoyed the game free of charge!

Fourteen years later there was a match by Wells' Light at Ewood Park for the benefit of Jack Southworth. Quite a big crowd turned up and saw the Rovers beat Darwen 2–0. In 1958 the club installed floodlights, first used on 10 November during a friendly against Werder Bremen. In 1976 the club up-graded the floodlights at a cost of £20,000. A friendly was arranged with Aberdeen, managed by former Rovers favourite, Ally MacLeod. Unfortunately, it was a dismal night and a crowd of under 4,000 meant the club recouped little of the initial outlay.

FA Cup

BLACKBURN ROVERS have won the FA Cup six times, a total equalled only by Arsenal and Newcastle United, and beaten only by Tottenham Hotspur (eight wins) and Aston Villa and Manchester United (seven wins).

It was only four years after their formation in 1875 that the Rovers first entered the FA Cup competition (then eight years old). By 1891—which is where the 'modern' Rovers story starts with the move from the Leamington Road ground to Ewood Park—the Rovers had been in six FA Cup finals and had won the trophy five times, three times in a row.

In fact, if one includes Rovers' old rivals, Olympic, the first provincial club to take the FA Cup, Blackburn was in seven finals out of ten between 1882 and 1891 and only once finished on the losing side.

Rovers first entered for the cup in 1879–80, one of fifty-four clubs. They beat Darwen 3–1 in the second round and then went out 6–0 to Nottingham Forest. In 1881–2 Rovers reached the final for the first time before being beaten 1–0 by Old Etonians at Kennington Oval in front of 7,000. Rovers were the first provincial club to reach the final, and a new era for soccer had been signalled.

But the Rovers' glory years were not at hand. Their town rivals Olympic beat them to the cup, winning it in 1883 by beating Old Etonians 2–1 after extra time.

The Rovers' first success came the following year when they beat Queen's Park Rangers, the famous Glasgow amateur side, 2–1 in the final. This was the first of a hat-trick of successes which was marked by the presentation to them by the Football Association of a silver shield. It still hangs in the Ewood Park boardroom—the club's most precious possession.

Queen's Park had a team of internationals—they were, to all intents and purposes, the Scottish national side at that time. With thirteen tried and trusty players available, the Rovers' committee had a ticklish job deciding their team for the final, but it included the 'mysterious' Fergie Suter, who fitted between Darwen and Blackburn. There was nothing mysterious about him at all—he was merely one of the first of the 'shamateurs'.

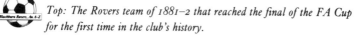 *Top: The Rovers team of 1881–2 that reached the final of the FA Cup for the first time in the club's history.*
Bottom: Rovers' first success came when they beat Queen's Park Rangers 2–1 in 1884.

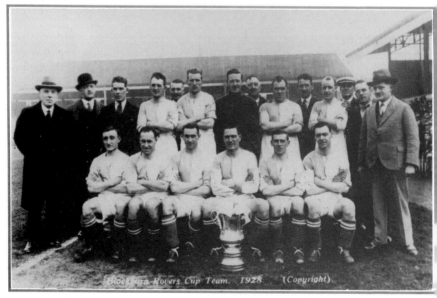

Top: The 1891 side that beat Notts County 3–1.
*Bottom: The 1928 side that beat Huddersfield 3–1 to take the Cup back
to Blackburn after an absence of thirty-seven years.*

A crowd of 12,000—a record at that time—watched the final, and Rovers' supporters were in such high spirits that the *Pall Mall Gazette* referred to them as 'a Northern horde of uncouth garb and strange oaths,' whose doings were likened to 'a tribe of Sudanese Arabs let loose.' Rovers won a famous match 2–1, where four more goals were disallowed by the referee.

Within twelve months the celebrations were repeated, for in 1885 the Rovers reached the final again, and once more their opponents were Queen's Park. Rovers won 2–0, the scorers being Jimmy Brown, their captain, and Jimmy Forrest, the first professional player to represent England against Scotland. In 1886, their fame now known throughout the land, Rovers were in their third successive final, and this time they needed two games before they beat West Brom.

In 1890 the Rovers were back at the Oval again for the first FA Cup final Battle of the Roses, their opponents being Sheffield Wednesday. Blackburn won 6–1, with William Townley grabbing a hat-trick. The following season the Rovers reaffirmed their position as one of the country's leading clubs when they retained the cup with a 3–1 victory over Notts County.

In 1893 and 1894 the Rovers reached the semi-final stage, but never did it again for seventeen years. The Rovers reached the semi-final in 1910–11 and 1911–12, when they found compensation for defeat by winning the championship, which they did again in 1914.

After the First World War the Rovers reached the semi-final in 1925, but at Wembley on 21 April 1928 they carried off the cup by beating Huddersfield Town 3–1. It was a match full of thrills from the very first minute, when Roscamp laid the foundation for Rovers' triumph with a goal, followed twenty-two minutes later by a second one from the foot of McLean. A desperate rally in the second half saw the hopes of the Yorkshiremen reduce the arrears, but the Rovers fought on with grim determination, Roscamp crowning his first success with another goal. Thus, after thirty-seven years, the cup went back to Blackburn.

On 6 March 1929 Ewood's record crowd of 61,783 saw the Rovers held by Bolton in the sixth round of the FA Cup, the Wanderers winning the replay 2–1. On 8 March 1947 the distinction of playing in the first FA Cup tie—other than the final—to be televised fell to the Ewood club when they met Charlton at The Valley in the fifth round.

Although the team struggled in the league, they reached the semi-final in 1951–2, losing to Newcastle United in a replay. They reached the semi-final stage again in 1957–8, only to lose 2–1 to Bolton Wanderers at Maine Road.

Rovers' last appearance in an FA Cup final came on 7 May 1960. Yet, incredibly, even before the team took to the field against Wolves, the Wembley dream had disintegrated into a nightmare. There was uproar over the distribution of tickets, causing a major rift between the club and its supporters. Meanwhile, Derek Dougan chose the journey down to London as the time to hand in a transfer request. The Wembley jinx struck when Dave Whelan broke and leg, and from that moment the game only had one winner. In one of the most boring of Wembley finals, Rovers went down 3–0.

Football League Cup

SAD TO RELATE, the Rovers have failed to make much impact upon the Football League (later Milk, Littlewoods, Rumbelows and Coca Cola) Cup, with the exception of 1961–2—and, of course, last season, when the club reached the semi-finals.

In 1961–2 Rovers battled their way through five rounds to reach the semi-finals before they were tumbled out by humble Rochdale over two legs! Then, as now, Rovers were a top-flight club. Rochdale were in the Fourth Division, but managed to pull off a major upset. It did not make too many headlines, for the competition wasn't taken seriously at the time. One of the highlights came in the second-round replay against Bristol Rovers at Ewood when Eddie Thomas scored all four goals in Blackburn's 4–0 win. At Spotland, in the first leg, Rovers were beaten 3–1 and, clearly, faced an uphill struggle in the return. A crowd of 11,644 saw goals from Pickering (pen) and Douglas give them a 2–1 victory, but it wasn't enough for the club to progress to the final.

Having been beaten by another 'little club', Wrexham, in the first season of the competition, these two experiences were a foretaste of things to come over the next three decades.

But last season the Rovers once again reached the semi-final stage. For many Blackburn fans, playing League cup ties in the New Year

The programme cover for last season's first-leg semi-final match against Sheffield Wednesday.

was a new experience, for many thought this competition came to an end in September or October!

It was during last season's run that the club's best scoreline in the League Cup was established when Rovers beat Watford at Ewood Park on 9 December 1992 by 6–1. Sheffield Wednesday were the club's opponents in the semi-final, but after Rovers had taken an early lead they were torn apart by the visitors. The deficit proved too great to pull back at Hillsborough, despite a brave attempt encouraged by Patrik Andersson's goal.

Rovers' record to date in the League Cup is:

P	W	D	L	F	A
100	40	24	36	157	144

Foreign Players

JOHN ROBERTS, an international goalkeeper from Australia, played for the Rovers in 1965–6. In the penultimate match of the season against Manchester United, in which Rovers lost 1–4 and were relegated, John Roberts was injured and, though he played his part in the club's Central League success the following season, he never returned to first-team duty.

Ben Arentoft, signed from Newcastle United for £15,000, was converted from mid-field to full-back with great success. He went on to make 108 first-team appearances before returning to his homeland, Denmark, to take up a business career.

The debut in a Rovers' shirt of Argentinian international Osvaldo Ardilles away at Plymouth on 26 March 1988 saw the now Tottenham manager put out of action by current Ewood starlet, Nicky Marker.

Perhaps the Rovers most unusual signing was Roy Wegerle. South African-born, playing in England, but qualified through marriage for the United States, Wegerle pledged himself to the Stars and Stripes and was an instant success. In 1992–3 the mid-season recruitment of Patrik Andersson (Sweden) and Henning Berg (Norway) brought a touch of the Viking influence to Ewood Park. Andersson played for

Sweden in the 1992 European Championships, while Berg played for Norway against England at Wembley.

The Rovers have had on their books some players who, though not born on foreign shores, had very foreign-sounding names—notably Kopel, Svarc and De Vries.

Jimmy Forrest

A TAPE-SIZER in the cotton trade, Jimmy Forrest holds a unique position among all the players who have worn the famous blue and white shirts of Blackburn Rovers. When he appeared in the 1891 FA Cup final he became the only man to have played in all five of the Rovers' triumphant cup final teams of the late nineteenth century.

An intelligent player who used his keen positional sense to enable him to intercept the ball, rather than having to rely on tackling to win possession, Jimmy Forrest was the first professional footballer to play for England, aged nineteen in 1886. His selection made history, and great controversy of protest from both sides of the border. He played in a tight-fitting shirt that distinguished him from the other twenty-one

Jimmy Forrest: the only man to have played in all five of Rovers' triumphant cup final teams of the late nineteenth century.

amateurs wearing loose jerseys—an imposition insisted on by H. L. Jackson.

He received £1 for his services on that occasion, and when the Rovers' committee heard of it they stopped his pay for a week!

Full Members' Cup Final

IT WOULD BE IMPOSSIBLE to over-estimate the importance of the occasion to Blackburn Rovers and their supporters. For not only did it give the club a chance to rescue a disappointing season, it also offered the opportunity to lay to rest the ghost of the FA Cup final some twenty-seven years earlier.

How they got there

Round 1   *Huddersfield Town 1 Blackburn Rovers 2*

In what was to be the club's only away tie in the competition, goals from Brotherston and Quinn were enough to defeat the Yorkshire side on a freezing cold night at Leeds Road.

Round 2   *Blackburn Rovers 1 Sheffield United 0*

Though the Blades played well on the night, it was a Simon Garner goal that gave Rovers their first win in eleven games.

Round 3   *Blackburn Rovers 4 Oxford United 3*

Simon Garner scored the only goal of the first half of this seven-goal thriller against First Division opposition. Two goals early in the second half put the visitors into the lead, but Glenn Keeley popped up to equalise. Whitehurst scored again for Oxford, but the Rovers still didn't die and Simon Barker equalised from the penalty spot after Scott Sellars had been brought down. With just three minutes remaining, Ainscow and Miller were brought on. Miller made ground and crossed for Ainscow to score with a brilliant diving header—his one touch of the game!

| Round 4 | *Blackburn Rovers 3 Chelsea 0* |

After a goal-less first half, Curry, Garner and Miller all scored to destroy the Pensioners, holders of the trophy.

| Semi-final | *Blackburn Rovers 3 Ipswich Town 0* |

After an edgy start, Simon Garner settled things down with a goal in the twenty-third minute and Simon Barker converted a penalty some fourteen minutes later following a clash between Garner and Cranson. Though Ipswich battled back well, Mark Patterson cleverly flicked the ball over Hallworth to make it 3–0.

| Final | *Blackburn Rovers 1 Charlton Athletic 0* |

The game itself was almost a non-event. Vince O'Keefe, the Rovers' number two goalkeeper, became an instant hero as he made a number of fine saves to keep Blackburn in the game. With the prospect of extra time looming, Ian Miller's perfect cross to the far side of the area tempted Bolder, the Charlton 'keeper, off his line, but he could only get his fingertips to it and the ball fell to Colin Hendry. The big blonde striker sent in a superb angled shot off the inside of the near post and into the net for the only goal of the game. The cup was presented to Glenn Keeley, who made his only mistake of the day and dropped it!

On the Monday evening the team returned to the town for a civic reception and were given an ecstatic welcome by thousands of fans. For a brief moment, the burden of Rovers' past glories had been lifted as at last the Blackburn public had something to celebrate.

Ken Furphy

KEN FURPHY was one of the new breed of tracksuit managers—an FA staff coach and a man of proven experience in handling clubs with limited resources. In fact, he was player-manager of Workington when the Cumbrian outfit brought about one of Rovers' most embarrassing Football League Cup exits.

Appointed in July 1971, he was to embark on the biggest rebuilding programme the club had ever experienced. The first few months of Furphy's first season in charge saw a procession of players coming and going, and although the Rovers enjoyed a record-breaking unbeaten run of nineteen games, they missed promotion by a couple of points.

Furphy made a good impression at Ewood and it came as no surprise when First Division Sheffield United offered him the vacant managership. Within a short time of leaving Ewood, he had returned to take Bradford, Field and Garbett with him to Bramall Lane.

Though he hadn't achieved success in terms of promotion while at Ewood, he made the club and supporters realise that their past glories counted for little when struggling in the Third Division. It was Furphy's period of reconstruction that provided the foundations for the club's future success. Unfortunately, though, Furphy's own career was on the wane. He was sacked by Sheffield United in October 1975 following a string of poor results, and so joined the exodus to the United States. He held various posts with New York Cosmos, Detroit Express and Washington Diplomats before returning to these shores in 1981.

Simon Garner

ARRIVING AT Ewood Park as a schoolboy in the summer of 1976, Simon Garner impressed both the Youth and Central League sides before making his first-team debut at the age of eighteen in a League Cup match at Exeter. A few days later he made his league debut when he appeared as a substitute at Newcastle. Originally he was used in

The programme cover for Simon Garner's testimonial year.

mid-field, but during the promotion campaign of 1979–80 manager Howard Kendall successfully converted him to inside-forward, where he formed a great partnership with Andy Kennedy for the last third of that season. It was during Kendall's reign as manager that Garner almost joined Halifax Town for a fee somewhere in the region of £40,000 but, fortunately for Rovers, he was reluctant to move.

When Bob Saxton replaced Kendall as manager, Garner seemed to find a new lease of life, his pace and power making him a handful for the Second Division defences. He capitalised on many defensive errors, notably the mis-timed back-passes that many defenders rued.

In 1982–3 he scored twenty-two league goals—it was his best season. On 10 September 1983 Simon Garner scored all five goals, including a penalty, as Rovers beat Derby County 5–1 in a Second Division match at Ewood Park. He hit another hat-trick towards the end of that season as Blackburn beat Portsmouth 4–2 at Fratton Park.

During the 1980s Garner won recognition as one of the deadliest marksmen outside of the First Division. At the start of the 1986–7 season he scored four goals as Blackburn beat Sunderland 6–1. Another hat-trick followed on 3 September 1988 as Rovers beat Lancashire neighbours Oldham 3–1.

He established a goal-scoring record for Blackburn Rovers that season. He took his aggregate total to 144 goals to overhaul the record set by Tommy Briggs of 140 league goals between 1952 and 1958. The record came in the match against Manchester City. If he scored more than one goal he would create history, having scored more league goals than any other player in the club's history. He scored in the thirteenth minute and almost broke the record early in the second half after having a shot cleared off the line, after nutmegging the City 'keeper. After seventy-four minutes the record was broken. Moving to the left of the penalty area, he hit a beautiful cross shot into the far side of the net. For good measure, three minutes later he completed his hat-trick, Rovers winning 4–0. Garner finished the season with twenty goals, his second best total.

It remained a mystery why no First Division club came in for him. Having come close to promotion for a number of years, the club finally made it in 1991–2, Simon Garner remaining loyal to the Rovers until his transfer to West Bromwich Albion in 1992, where his goal-scoring exploits have continued to prove so valuable, taking the Throstles to the play-offs and eventually the First Division.

Glossop North East

GLOSSOP NORTH EAST won promotion to the First Division at the end of their first season in the league, 1898–9. The following season they beat the Rovers 4–2 at home and drew 2–2 at Ewood Park. In spite of this they were relegated, and spent the rest of the time in the lower division. They finished bottom of the table in the last season before the First World War, 1914–15, and resigned from the leagues shortly before the resumption of matches in 1919.

Goalkeepers

BLACKBURN ROVERS have almost always been extremely well served by their goalkeepers, and most of them have been highly popular with the supporters.

Thomas Greenwood was the club's first captain and goalkeeper, whilst T. Wilkie, another of Rovers' earliest 'keepers, was so dreadful, losing his bearings so completely that he 'failed to distinguish his team-mates from the opposition'. In trying to find a goalkeeper for the 1889–90 season, the club headed north of the border to sign Neg Doig for thirty sovereigns: a typical Rovers signing, he played one game, a 9–1 victory over Notts County, before returning home.

Herbie Arthur, goalkeeper for the cup-winning sides of 1884, '85 and '86, only agreed to re-sign for the Rovers on the condition that he was made captain. Arthur's other claim to fame came in a match against Burnley when his team-mates walked off because of the intense cold. Herbie was made of sterner stuff and faced the eleven of Burnley alone. When Burnley kicked-off, however, he kept appealing for offside, with the result that the referee finally abandoned the game.

A mammoth figure, Jack 'Tiny' Joyce was a goalkeeper who paid little attention to the accepted conventions. He loathed inactivity and would enliven proceedings by dashing up-field in pursuit of the ball. He considered catching the ball a waste of seconds, and so would cock a steel-hard wrist and despatch the ball vast distances up-field. In

addition, he considered himself a penalty expert, though the Rovers would never indulge his whims.

One of the bravest of Rovers' goalkeepers was Ronnie Sewell who, during a match in the 1920s, was treated for a suspected broken wrist. The referee restarted play before Sewell had replaced his jersey and the first attack was repulsed bare-chested. In the final minute of the game he collided with the post, knocking himself out!

The record for the longest period from a goalkeeper's debut to conceding his first goal is held by Bill Hughes, who was within a minute of keeping a clean sheet for his first three games in the 1948–9 season.

One of the best goalkeepers the club has ever had, Reg Elvy's arrival at Ewood Park was purely fortuitous. The club were bottom of the Second Division and Patterson, the first-team 'keeper, had broken his arm in a practice game and officials dashed to Bolton to sign the Lancashire cricketer, Ken Grieves. Instead, they came back with Elvy, a signing they were soon to congratulate themselves on. In five seasons he missed only three league games, and two of these were at the very end when it had been decided to give him a free transfer.

Fred Else, signed from Preston North End for £20,000, was the first Rovers goalkeeper to wear the number one on his jersey.

The record for the longest unbeaten spell between one goal and the next conceded by a goalkeeper is held by Adam Blacklaw with 582 minutes, which covered a period at the end of the 1968–9 season and the start of the 1969–70 season; whilst until last season Jim Arnold held the record for the greatest number of 'clean sheets' in a season—nineteen in 1979–80.

Roger Jones, signed for £30,000 from Bournemouth in January 1970, went on to break the club's record for goalkeeping appearances until Terry Gennoe—the only Rovers 'keeper to be sent off—beat it. His total of 289 Football League appearances is the current club record for a goalkeeper.

Rovers' present goalkeeper, Bobby Mimms, wrote his name in the Ewood record books last season with more 'clean sheets' than any other Rovers 'keeper in a top-flight campaign—nineteen in forty-two Premier League games.

Goalscoring

For the club

The Rovers' highest goal-scoring tallies were achieved in 1954–5 when the team finished sixth in the Second Division and scored 114 league goals in forty-two matches, and in 1929–30 when the club scored 99 goals to finish sixth in the First Division.

For the individual

The following players have scored fifty or more league goals for the club:

Simon Garner	(1978–92)	168
Tommy Briggs	(1952–58)	140
Ted Harper	(1923–58)	121
Jack Bruton	(1929–39)	108
Bryan Douglas	(1954–69)	100
Jack Southworth	(1887–93)	97
Eddie Latheron	(1906–15)	94
Eddie Quigley	(1951–56)	92
Andy McEvoy	(1958–67)	89
Peter Dobing	(1956–61)	88
Jack Thompson	(1931–37)	82
Syd Puddefoot	(1924–32)	79
Wattie Aitkenhead	(1906–15)	75
Eddie Crossan	(1947–57)	73
Percy Dawson	(1913–23)	71
Billy Davies	(1905–12)	66
Fred Pickering	(1959–63)	61

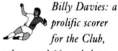

Billy Davies: a prolific scorer for the Club, who netted 66 goals between 1905 and 1912.

Danny Shea	(1912–20)	61
Don Martin	(1967–76)	58
Bobby Langton	(1938–56)	57
Arnold Whittaker	(1899–1908)	57
John Byrom	(1961–77)	50
Harry Chippendale	(1891–7)	50

All dates refer to calendar years of debuts and last appearances.
Correct to August 1993.

'Golden Goal' Tickets

IN ONE OF THE final home games of the 1970–1 season, Rovers desperately needed a win against Millwall. After missing a twice-taken penalty, Rovers conceded two goals which virtually condemned them to the Third Division for the first time. The second goal scored by Eamonn Dunphy was a unique one. At the time the Development Association was raising funds by selling 'Golden Goal' tickets, giving a player's number and a time. For the holder to win, a goal had to be scored by that player at the time stated. Dunphy purchased a ticket, which he later found read 'Visitors number ten, eighty-eighth minute'. The number was his own, and in precisely that minute he slotted the second goal into the net.

Guest Players

THE 'GUEST' SYSTEM was used by all clubs during the two wars. Although at times it was abused almost beyond belief (some sides that opposed Blackburn had ten or eleven 'guests'!), it normally worked sensibly and effectively to the benefit of the players, clubs and supporters. During the First World War many of the Rovers' staff drifted to Lancashire clubs who were willing to field sides in the league. George Chapman, Albert Walmsley, Arthur Cowell and Johnny Orr turned out for Burnley, whilst Wattie Aitkenhead and Tom Suttie represented Preston and Accrington Stanley respectively. Bob Crompton, along with Latheron and Hodkinson, sampled the sea air at Blackpool, while other players returned to their native towns. The great Jocky Simpson assisted Falkirk, and Danny Shea began to appear for West Ham, Fulham, Birmingham City and Notts Forest.

When the Rovers visited Stoke City they had to borrow Underwood, a goalkeeper, from their hosts. He conceded sixteen goals! The following fortnight the only person available was a Liverpool boxer named Best. He conceded seven goals, but played extremely well!

Perhaps the best known of Rovers' 'guest' players were Preston's mighty little centre-half Joe McCall, who dropped in for one game, and Tom Brandon's son Harold, who made several appearances. In the Second World War George Mutch, the Manchester United and Preston North End forward, 'guested' on a couple of occasions, though it was Tommy Pearson of Newcastle United who ran the left wing with verve and sparkle and brought the spectators to Ewood Park. He was rewarded with the crowd's worship or, at least, as much idolising as the times allowed.

Above and opposite: Jocky Simpson and Danny Shea, two players who 'guested' for other clubs during the First World War. Simpson was with Falkirk and Shea with West Ham, Fulham, Birmingham and Nottingham Forest.

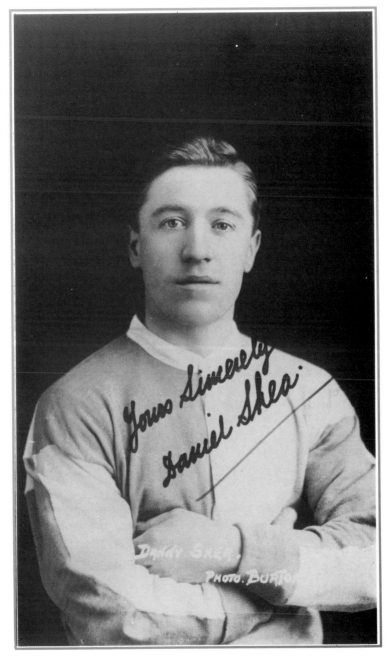

Halifax Town

THE SHAYMEN lost their Football League status at the end of the 1992–3 season. Having played their first football league game on 27 August 1921 in the Third Division (North), the club enjoyed sixty-five seasons without ever winning a League Championship.

The Rovers met Halifax for four consecutive seasons in the Third Division from 1971–2. In that first season the Rovers completed the double over their Yorkshire opponents, 2–0 at Ewood and 1–0 at the Shay. While never achieving the double over the next three seasons, Blackburn never lost to Halifax, winning four and drawing four of their eight encounters.

William Townley: the first man to score a hat-trick in an FA Cup Final.

Hat-tricks

THE CLUB'S FIRST hat-trick in the Football League came from Jack Southworth in the 7–1 win at Burnley on 3 November 1888. He was the king of the hat-tricks and scored twelve in a Rovers career that was cut short by his transfer to Everton.

Not surprisingly, Ted Harper and Andy McEvoy, two of the

best goal-scorers the club has ever had, are next on the list with eight hat-tricks. Also high up on the list is Fred Pickering with five, his partnership with McEvoy being one of the most prolific the club has produced.

The only Blackburn player to score a hat-trick on his debut for the club was Arnold Whittaker, who scored all three in the 3–0 home defeat of Preston North End on 14 October 1899. For his pains he was greeted warmly by the North End goal-keeper, McBride. Unfortunately for Whittaker, the glowering

Jack Southworth: the scorer of the Club's first hat-trick in the Football League.

McBride was not one for bestowing handshakes. Instead, he selected Whittaker's throat!

When Blackburn won the FA Cup in 1889–90, William Townley created a record when he became the first man to hit a hat-trick in an FA Cup final as Rovers beat Sheffield Wednesday 6–1.

The only hat-trick scored by a Rovers player in the Football League Cup is by Eddie Thomas, who scored all four goals in Blackburn's 4–0 home win over Bristol Rovers in a second round replay on 16 October 1961.

There have been six occasions when *two* Rovers players have scored hat-tricks in the same match. The first came in 1888–9 when R. Haresnape (3) and Southworth (4) helped Rovers to an 8–1 home win over Aston Villa in the FA Cup. The first instance in the Football League came in 1890–1 when Coombe Hall (4) and Southworth (3) scored in Rovers' 8–0 home win against Derby County. In 1894–5, Harry Chippendale and Killean scored three apiece in Rovers' 9–1 win at

Ewood over Small Heath. In 1913–14 Rovers beat Middlesbrough 6–0 with Jock Cameron and Danny Shea scoring hat-tricks. In 1954–5 Eddie Quigley and Frank Mooney scored three goals apiece in the 9–0 thrashing of Middlesbrough, while the last occasion occurred in 1963–4 as Fred Pickering and Andy McEvoy scored hat-tricks in Rovers' best away win in the Football League—8–2 at West Ham.

The only occasion when a player has scored a double hat-trick came in Rovers' 8–3 win over Bristol Rovers on 5 February 1955, when Tommy Briggs scored seven of the goals, though G. Chapman scored all six in the 6–1 home win over Rochdale in the 1916–17 Lancashire Section (Principal Tournament).

The last Blackburn player to score a hat-trick was David Speedie, who hit all three in Rovers' 3–1 win against Plymouth Argyle at Home Park on 2 May 1992. Speedie is also the last player to score a hat-trick at Ewood Park when Rovers beat Newcastle United 3–1 on 15 February 1992.

Home Matches

NOT INCLUDING the pre-Football League matches, Rovers' best *home wins* were the 9–0 rout of Middlesbrough in a Division Two match on 6 November 1954, and 9–1 victories over Notts County in a football League match on 16 November 1889 and their neighbours Notts Forest in a Division Two match on 10 April 1937.

In 1889–90 Rovers beat Stoke 8–0 and repeated the scoreline the following season against Derby County. In Blackburn's first season in the Football League they beat Aston Villa 8–1 in the third round of the FA Cup and then Sunderland by the same score in season 1908–9. Rovers scored eight goals in two other home matches, beating Burnley in 1929–30 and Bristol Rovers in 1954–5 by the same 8–3 margin.

More recently, Blackburn beat Norwich City 7–1, one of eighteen occasions that the Rovers have scored seven goals in a home fixture. They kept a clean sheet on six of these occasions: Aston Villa 1889–90; Chester 1890–1; Woolwich Arsenal 1909–10; Manchester United 1925–6; Middlesbrough 1929–30; and Doncaster Rovers 1954–5.

Rovers' worst home defeat has been 1–7, on two occasions—against Notts County on 14 March 1891 and against Middlesbrough on 29 November 1947.

The highest scoring home match other than those mentioned above is Rovers' 7–5 victory over Birmingham City on 28 September 1929—it was a season when Rovers won by the same scoreline at Bramall Lane on 3 March 1930!

Home Seasons

BLACKBURN ROVERS have gone through a complete league season with an undefeated home record on four occasions:

1888–9	Football League	won 7	drew 4
1909–10	Division One	won 13	drew 6
1911–12	Division One	won 13	drew 6
1933–4	Division One	won 16	drew 5

Rovers' highest number of home wins in a League season is seventeen. They achieved this number of victories in 1938–9 from a twenty-one-match programme.

The nearest the club has come to an undefeated home record in recent years was 1983–4, when the side's only defeat came at the hands of Fulham (0–1) on 29 April 1984.

International Players

ROVER'S most capped player (i.e. caps gained while players were registered with the club) is Bob Crompton with forty-one caps. The following is a complete list of players who have gained full international honours while at Ewood Park:

England	caps	Scotland	caps
J. W. H. Arthur	7	W. C. A. Aitkenhead	1
J. Beverley	3	T. Brandon	1
J. Barton	1	J. Hutton	3
F. Blackburn	3	J. McKay	1
T. Booth	1		
W. Bradshaw	4	*Wales*	
J. Brown	6	W. Davies	9
A. F. Campbell	2	M. H. England	20
H. Chippendale	1	R. O. Evans	1
R. Clayton	35	B. Hole	7
A. Cowell	1	J. I. Hughes	1
R. Crompton	41	W. A. Hughes	5
A. Cunliffe	2	R. T. Vernon	9
B. Douglas	36		
W. Eckersley	17	*Northern Ireland*	
J. H. Forrest	11	N. Brotherston	27
D. H. Greenwood	2	E. Crossan	3
F. W. Hargreaves	3	D. Dougan	5
J. Hargreaves	2	A. Hunter	6
E. C. Harper	1	I. Lawther	2
H. Healless	2	J. Quinn	13
J. Hodkinson	3	P. Robinson	1
A. E. Houlker	1	D. Rollo	12
H. Jones	6		
R. Langton	7	*Republic of Ireland*	
E. G. Latheron	2	J. Haverty	2
J. M. Lofthouse	7	M. A. McEvoy	17
K. R. Newton	20	M. McGrath	18
S. C. Puddefoot	2	K. Moran	20
A. Rigby	5	E. Rogers	14
W. R. Sewell	1	F. Stapleton	2
D. Shea	2		
A. Shearer	3		
J. Simpson	8	Rovers' first player to be capped was Fred Hargreaves, who played for England v. Wales on 15 March 1880.	
Jack Southworth	3		
W. J. Townley	2		
N. Walton	1		
J. Whitehead	1		

Howard Kendall

HOWARD KENDALL proved to be one of the most successful managers in the club's history. As a player, he created football history on May 1964 when, still twenty days short of his eighteenth birthday, he became the youngest player to appear in an FA Cup final. In March 1967 Everton paid Preston North End a fee of £80,000 for his services. At Goodison he became a member of the legendary mid-field trio of Kendall, Ball and Harvey. Yet, despite his acclaimed performances, international honours eluded him throughout his career. In February 1974 he moved to Birmingham City, where he helped to stabilise them in the First Division and take them to the 1975 FA Cup semi-final. Two years later he moved to Stoke City and became the club coach as the Potters won promotion to Division One in 1978–9.

Howard Kendall arrived at Ewood in the 1979 close season as Rovers were still suffering from one of the most traumatic seasons in their history. Despite a poor start to the 1979–80 season, Kendall soon moulded a team together.

The club's success was based on a firm foundation. Jim Arnold, a goalkeeper from Stafford Rangers, was signed, while Branagan, Keeley, Fazackerley and Rathbone proved to be one of the best defensive units outside the First Division. Kendall and Tony Parkes commanded the mid-field, while the superb skills of Duncan McKenzie wrought havoc on opposition defence. Kendall led the Rovers through an incredible run of games to gain promotion to the Second Division.

The following campaign saw Kendall once again lead his side to the top of the division, and, though mean defending was the route he took to gain success, it was the club's lack of goals that proved to be Kendall's undoing, as Swansea City pipped Blackburn for promotion on goal-difference.

It was at Everton where Kendall experienced his finest days as a player, so when the Goodison Park outfit came in for his services, the pull of Everton proved too strong.

He didn't achieve instant success on Merseyside, but after winning a Milk Cup tie at Oxford he never looked back—the FA Cup, European Cup-winners' Cup and the League Championship were all won

under Kendall's leadership. In June 1987 he turned his back on English football to join the Spanish club Athletic Bilbao. After a run of poor results he was sacked, but on his return to England was appointed manager of Manchester City. When Everton decided to terminate Colin Harvey's contract it was Kendall they approached, and so, in November 1990, he joined the Toffees for a second spell as manager.

Lancashire Manx Cup

THE LANCASHIRE CUP was purchased originally in 1878 for £160 and first won by Darwen FC, who defeated the Rovers 3–0 before a crowd of 9,000 with gate receipts of £167.

The cup is a staggering 3 ft. 3 ins. high and carries some beautifully created ornate features which make it a truly outstanding work of art.

Blackburn Rovers have won the trophy on fifteen occasions, the most successful of all Lancashire clubs. Burnley and Manchester United are the next most successful clubs, but also on the list of winners are former Football League clubs Accrington, Barrow and, of course, Darwen.

For the past eleven seasons the Isle of Man Department of Tourism have sponsored the competition and this has enabled Lancashire clubs to benefit financially from competitive pre-season games.

The Rovers have four victories in the newly sponsored cup competition:

1983	Bury	Home	0–0	(3–1 on penalties)
1985	Burnley	Home	1–0	
1987	Wigan Athletic	Home	2–2	(4–3 on penalties)
1989	Blackpool	Away	1–0	

Bobby Langton

BOBBY LANGTON was a promising teenager who signed for Blackburn Rovers for just £50 from Southport League side Burscough Victoria in 1937. At the time he was only eighteen years old, but was quickly installed into the outside-left position, from where he scored fourteen goals in thirty-seven appearances during Rovers' promotion campaign of 1938–9. His First Division appearances were restricted to three, scoring the second equaliser in the 2–2 draw with Everton in the last game before the outbreak of war interrupted his career.

During the war he was an infantryman in India and represented the army in practically every game they played during his service. He appeared in the 1940 War Cup final when Rovers lost 0–1 to West Ham. In 1945 he was a member of the Glentoran team that reached the Irish Cup final and also represented the Irish League against the Combined Services in Belfast.

The end of the war saw him restored to the Blackburn side, and in September 1946 he won his first cap for England against Northern Ireland. Blackburn's fortunes waned, and in August 1949 he was transferred to Preston North End for £16,000. In the same month he netted a goal after only seven seconds from the kick-off against Manchester City. In November 1949 Bobby Langton was on his way to Bolton Wanderers for what was then a club record fee of £20,000.

Langton was in his prime—possessing a very powerful shot, he liked to cut inside from the left and have a crack at goal. He was a speedy winger who could put in crosses from all angles.

At Bolton he became a regular in the number eleven shirt until 1953, when he was placed on the transfer list at his own request. He remained long enough to play in the 1953 FA Cup final against Blackpool. In September of that year he returned to Ewood Park.

Although his speed had diminished somewhat in his second spell at Blackburn, he added a great deal of guile and cunning to his play. In fact, during this time with Rovers he scored thirty-three goals from his 105 appearances.

After leaving league football he had a spell in Ireland with Ards, before entering non-league football with Kidderminster Harriers. His non-league career took him to Wisbech Town twice (where he became

a publican), and Colwyn Bay. In 1962 he became trainer-coach at King's Lynn and a year later took over a similar position at Wisbech. Five years later he returned to his roots, becoming manager of Burscough Rangers.

Largest Crowd

IT WAS ON 2 March 1929 that Ewood Park housed its largest crowd. The occasion was the FA Cup sixth round match against neighbours, Bolton Wanderers. The crowd was a staggering 61,783, the receipts £4,772, and the scoreline 1–1 with Jock Hutton grabbing the Rovers' goal.

Late Finishes to a Season

BLACKBURN'S play-off match against Crystal Palace at Selhurst Park on Sunday 4 June 1989 is the latest date for the finish of any Rovers season.

If the play-offs are excluded, Blackburn's latest finish to a league season was 26 May in the 1946–7 season, when a Wightman goal was enough to defeat Charlton Athletic at Ewood Park.

During the war many curious things occurred, and in 1939–40 Rovers contested the League War Cup final with West Ham on 8 June. The club's last match in the North West Regional League that season was on 3 June, when a Hargreaves hat-trick helped Rovers beat Rochdale 4–2.

Leading Goal-scorers

The ROVERS have provided the Football League's leading goal-scorer on a number of occasions. In 1890–1 Jack Southworth scored twenty-six goals in the Football League, while Ted Harper scored forty-three goals in 1925–6 as Rovers finished twelfth in the First Division. In 1954–5 Tommy Briggs headed the country's goal-scoring with thirty-three goals in the Second Division. Tommy Johnston topped the list in 1957–8 with forty-three strikes, though thirty-five of his goals were scored for Leyton Orient. The last Rovers player to head a league's goal-scoring chart is Andy McEvoy who, along with Jimmy Greaves in 1964–5, scored twenty-nine goals.

Leamington Street

THE GROUND at the top of Leamington Street was enclosed and well drained and had a slight fall. A 'handsome' and spacious grandstand was built, painted in the club colours, and seated 600.

Large crowds gathered on 15 October 1881 for the first game at Rovers' new venue. A local derby match was played with Blackburn Olympic providing the opposition. Rovers won 4–1 in front of a crowd of around 6,000. This first season at Leamington Street was to become the club's best to date, for after thrashing Park Road 9–1 in the first round of the FA Cup they caused a football sensation by becoming the first northern club to reach the final, when they lost by the only goal of the game at the Oval to the Old Etonians.

The club's stay at Leamington Street lasted for nine years, and this period represented one of the most successful in the club's history. Their honours included their winning of the FA Cup in three consecutive seasons, and their entry in 1888 to the first Football League in the world.

The club's league campaign started on 15 September with an amazing five-all draw at home to near neighbours Accrington. The team had a good season and finished fourth in the final league table. A number of friendly games followed, which culminated in a single-goal home defeat to non-league rivals Darwen on 17 May 1889.

There was no announcement that this was to be the club's last season at Leamington Street and, since it was reported that the ground was 'lost', it can be assumed that a move was not instigated by the club.

Gordon Lee

AS A PLAYER, Gordon Lee enjoyed a long and successful career with Aston Villa before moving to Shrewsbury Town as player-coach in 1966. He began his managerial career with Port Vale in 1968, taking them into the Third Division in 1971. He arrived at Ewood in January 1974 with hard work and dedication forming his foundations for success. However, within a short time it became clear that he felt a number of players did not share his simple philosophy, and so began another phase of rebuilding.

After assessing the relative merits of his squad, he began to accumulate the finance for his rebuilding programme. Having cleared the decks, Lee began to bring in new faces. Hilton on a free transfer and Beamish for £25,000—the biggest fee Lee had ever paid for a player—were brought in from Brighton. They were followed by Hawkins, Oates and Mullen; while Burgin, Hickman and Hoy all arrived at strategic moments in the season. However, it was under Gordon Lee that players like Stuart Metcalfe and Tony Parkes showed their true mettle in mid-field as the manager's fighting spirit rubbed off. Perhaps the most astute move was Lee's decision to resurrect the career of Don Martin, who was languishing in the Central League.

When Rovers won the title on May 1975, Lee became the centre of a controversial tug-of-war with Newcastle United; and the Ewood board discovered that yet again a contract was no protection against the lure of First Division football.

John Lewis

WHILE HISTORIANS referred to John Lewis as the chairman of the club from 1875–88, it is more than likely that he was, for the most part, the leader of the committee during this period, and certainly he acted as treasurer for some considerable time.

He was certainly the founder of Blackburn Rovers in as much that, along with Arthur Constantine, he was responsible for calling the meeting at the St Leger Hotel to put forward his ideas on the forming of a Blackburn club. He was known throughout football in the latter part of the nineteenth century as 'The Prince of Referees', having the unique honour of refereeing three FA Cup finals in 1895, 1897 and 1898.

John Lewis was also a founder and council member of the Lancashire Football Association. He went to the meeting held at the Volunteer Inn, Bromley Cross, near Bolton in 1878. As he was an advocate of teetotalism, it is quite amazing that

 John Lewis: the founder of the Blackburn Rovers.

both the forming of the Rovers and the Lancashire Football Association took place in public ale houses!

Known universally as 'Honest John', he became a member of the Football League Management Committee in 1894 for one season and was re-elected in 1900, serving for twenty-five years in total, and acting as vice-president of the Football League from 1901 to 1925.

In 1911 Lewis was appointed a Football Association councillor, and in 1923 he became vice-president of the Football Association, serving in that capacity until his death in 1926.

At his passing the Football Association stated,

> His influence on the game at home and abroad was immense and he pioneered the game of football not only through Great Britain and Ireland, but on the Continent, South Africa and Australia. A most remarkable man who left his mark in many directions and soccer will probably not see his like again.

Lowest

THE LOWEST NUMBER of goals scored by Blackburn Rovers in a single Football League season is thirty-five, in 1896–7. However, that was a thirty-match season, and in 1970–1, when the club was relegated to Division Three, only thirty-seven goals were scored.

The lowest points record in the Football League occurred in 1965–6, when Rovers gained just twenty points to finish bottom of the First Division.

Don Mackay

DURING HIS PLAYING DAYS, Don Mackay was a goalkeeper, beginning his career with Forfar Athletic. He was transferred to Dundee United in 1969 and made forty-nine league appearances for them before trying his luck in England with Southern United.

After hanging up his gloves he turned his attention to coaching and worked with Bristol City before accepting the manager's job at Dens Park, Dundee. After four years of success he was given the job at Coventry City. Two successful campaigns staving off relegation were followed by his dismissal in April 1986.

Don returned to Scotland to run the reserve and youth sides for Graeme Souness at Rangers. Then in February 1987 he was installed at Ewood Park, brought in to revive the fortunes of a team anchored at the foot of the Second Division table.

He changed the style of play to get more men forward and results began to come. He steered the Rovers to a Full Members' Cup victory beneath the twin towers and displayed boldness and courage in persuading the likes of Archibald and Ardilles to join the club.

Although promotion eluded him, Mackay certainly went some way to laying the accusation that Rovers lacked ambition.

His second full season at Ewood proved even more successful than the first, and though promotion eluded them again in the most heartbreaking of circumstances, the club was in a far healthier state than when he arrived at Blackburn.

The 1989–90 season saw Mackay bring in big-name players to Ewood Park. Frank Stapleton and Kevin Moran joined the staff, though his failure to strengthen the squad during the final run-in saw him under fire for the first time since his appointment.

A victim of his own success, having taken the club to the brink of the top flight on three successive occasions, he was sacked in 1991 before being appointed manager of Fulham.

Managers

THIS IS THE complete list of Rovers' full-time managers with the inclusive dates in which they held office. Biographies of those who have made major contributions to the club are included in alphabetical order.

Jack Carr	1922–6	Eddie Quigley	1967–70
Bob Crompton	1926–31	Johnny Carey	1970–1
Arthur Barrit	1931–6	Ken Furphy	1971–3
Reg Taylor	1936–8	Gordon Lee	1974–5
Bob Crompton	1938–41	Jim Smith	1975–8
Eddie Hapgood	1944–7	Jim Iley	1978
Will Scott	1947	John Pickering	1978–9
Jack Bruton	1947–9	Howard Kendall	1979–81
Jackie Bestall	1949–53	Bobby Saxton	1981–6
Johnny Carey	1953–8	Don Mackay	1987–91
Dally Duncan	1958–60	Kenny Dalglish	1991–
Jack Marshall	1960–7		

Marathon Match

IT WAS IN THE 1900–1 season that Blackburn Rovers and Bury, to decide a single tie in the Lancashire Cup, played each other in five matches. The first four matches were drawn, in spite of extra time, and, finally, Rovers won 3–1, again after extra time, at the fifth meeting at Burnden Park. Before the issue was decided, the two clubs had actually played eight hours and twenty-six minutes.

Jack Marshall

Jack Marshall: Rovers manager, 1960–7.

A PLAYER WITH Burnley before the war, Jack Marshall's career was cut short by injury and he joined the coaching staff at Bury. After a spell with Stoke City he moved to Sheffield Wednesday as head trainer, a position he also held with the England 'B' team. In September 1958 he moved to Spotland to become manager of Rochdale.

Replacing 'Dally' Duncan, Marshall joined Blackburn six matches into the 1960–1 season. Having assessed the playing strength, the new manager decided against wholesale changes, but made some important positional changes in his first two seasons in charge. Fred Pickering moved from full-back to centre-forward, Keith Newton settled in to full-back and Andy McEvoy was allowed to return to his original inside-forward position.

Against all the odds, Marshall kept the Rovers challenging for the First Division Championship as they played entertaining football. Unfortunately, though, like Johnny Carey's sides of the mid-1950s, the club was plagued by inconsistency.

In March 1964 Pickering was controversially sold to Everton, as Marshall's team began to break up. A disastrous 1965–6 campaign saw the Rovers drop into the Second Division and, as Marshall's contract had expired, many fans wondered if he would be given the chance to restore the club's fortunes. Though he was working on a week-to-week basis, Marshall began to rebuild the team, but in November 1966 Eddie Quigley was brought in as Marshall's assistant and given responsibility for coaching throughout the club. The erratic form of previous weeks continued and in February 1967, unhappy with several aspects of life at Ewood, Marshall tendered his resignation.

He returned to football as Alan Brown's assistant at Hillsborough, and when Brown and Wednesday parted company Marshall became manager. A year later he was told that his contract was not being renewed and he moved on to manage Bury. In July 1970 he returned to Ewood Park as physiotherapist, before finally retiring to his native Bolton in 1979.

Missionaries

DURING 1894–5 M. Calvey became the first of many old Rovers to spread the Association gospel abroad when he left for America to teach the Americans football. Others included Edgar Chadwick in Czechoslovakia and Germany; Bill Gormlie in Belgium; James Donnelly in Yugoslavia and Italy; Billy Garbutt in Italy; Frank Crawley in the United States and Canada; and Les Talbot, Harry Healless and Walter Crook in Holland. One of the younger boys Crook taught to kick a ball correctly during his stay at Ajax was a youngster by the name of Johann Cruyff!

Most Goals in a Season

BLACKBURN ROVERS scored 114 goals in forty-two Division Two matches during the 1954–5 season. They only failed to score in two home games and one away game. Seventy-three goals came at home, and in ten games four or more goals were scored.

At Ewood Park Middlesbrough were beaten 9–0, Bristol Rovers 8–3 and Doncaster Rovers 7–0, though the Rovers lost 3–7 at Luton Town.

The top scorer was Tommy Briggs with thirty-three goals (including seven in the victory over Bristol Rovers), while Eddie Quigley had twenty-eight. Blackburn finished the season in sixth place.

Most Matches

IN THE SPACE OF three weeks in the month of April 1894, the Rovers played the following matches:

April 7	Linfield Athletic	Home	Won	4–0
9	Darwen	Away	Won	2–1
11	Celtic	Away	Drew	0–0
12	Liverpool	Away	Won	5–0
13	Burnley	Home	Lost	1–2
14	Stoke City	Home	Won	5–0
15	Heart of Midlothian	Away	Lost	1–2
17	East Stirling	Away	Won	3–1
18	Wishaw Thistle	Away	Won	10–2
19	Preston North End	Home	Lost	0–2
20	Burnley	Away	Lost	1–2
20	Accrington (ELCC)	Away	Drew	1–1
21	Preston North End	Away	Lost	0–6

23	Darwen	Home	Won	4–0
24	Liverpool	Away	Won	3–1
25	Southport Central	Away	Won	2–1
26	Accrington (ELCC)	Home	Won	4–0
28	Bolton Wanderers	Away	Won	4–0

And before all that, of course, the Rovers had gone through the formality of winning the FA Cup five times!

Neutral Grounds

EWOOD PARK has been used as a neutral ground for FA Cup matches on a number of occasions, and as early as April 1891 staged an international match between England and Scotland. Thousands of spectators stayed away from the game as there was no Rovers player in the side. England won 2–1 with the second goal scored by Everton's Edgar Chadwick, a native of Blackburn.

In 1893 the ground was awarded its first FA Cup semi-final, a replay between Everton and Preston North End, while two years later Wales and England drew 1–1 at international level. In February 1910 Ewood was the venue for a Football League representative game against the Scottish League, while later that year England met Scotland.

On 29 March 1913 Aston Villa beat Oldham Athletic by the only goal of the game in the FA Cup semi-final at Ewood, and then on 27 March 1915 Sheffield United defeated Bolton Wanderers 2–1 at the same stage of the competition. On Monday 3 March 1924 Wales met England on a snow-covered ground at Ewood Park. No goals were scored in the first half, but after Roberts had scored for England, Davies and Vizard both scored to give Wales victory by 2–1. One of the incidents of this match was the bursting of the ball. Tommy Roberts, leading the England attack, sent in one of his then-famous shots from outside the penalty area. The ball crashed against the cross bar of the Blackburn end goal and came almost straight down, burst by the impact.

In March 1938 Ewood Park was the venue for another FA Cup semi-final when Huddersfield Town defeated Sunderland 3–1. On 31 May 1941 Ewood Park housed the Football League War Cup final between Preston North End and Arsenal. The last major representative game at the ground was the Football League *v* League of Ireland, while in 1947 Burnley played Liverpool at Ewood in the semi-final of the FA Cup.

The Rovers themselves have had to replay on a neutral ground a number of times:

Date	Opponents	Venue	FA Cup stage	Score
15 March 1882	Sheffield Wednesday	Manchester	Semi-final	5–1
10 April 1886	West Brom Albion	Derby	Final	2–0
23 March 1889	Wolves	Crewe	Semi-final	1–3
5 Feb. 1900	Portsmouth	Villa Park	Round 2	5–0
11 Feb. 1907	Tottenham Hotspur	Villa Park	Round 2	1–2
3 April 1912	West Brom Albion	Sheffield	Semi-final	0–1
9 Feb. 1925	Portsmouth	Highbury	Round 2	1–0
20 Feb. 1939	Sunderland	Hillsborough	Round 5	1–0
2 April 1952	Newcastle United	Elland Road	Semi-final	1–2

The club's semi-finals were, of course, played on neutral grounds. In the pre-league seasons 1879 to 1888, Rovers were involved in four FA Cup semi-finals. The first of these, on 6 March 1882, was a goal-less draw against Sheffield Wednesday at Huddersfield Rugby Club, Rovers winning the replay at Manchester 5–1. In March 1884 Rovers beat Notts County 2–1 at Birmingham; in March 1885 Old Carthusians 5–1 at Nottingham and in 1886 Swifts 2–1 at Derby as the club went on to win the FA Cup three years in succession. The full list of Rovers' appearances in an FA Cup semi-final on a neutral ground in their league days is as follows:

Date	Opponents	Venue	Score
16 March 1889	Wolves	Alexandra Ground, Crewe	1–1
8 March 1890	Wolves	Wrexham	1–0

Date	Opponents	Venue	Score
28 February 1891	West Brom Albion	Stoke	3–3
4 March 1893	Wolves	Nottingham	1–2
10 March 1894	Notts County	Bramall Lane	0–1
25 March 1911	Bradford City	Bramall Lane	0–3
30 March 1912	West Brom Albion	Anfield	0–0
28 March 1925	Cardiff City	Nottingham	1–3
24 March 1928	Arsenal	Leicester	1–0
29 March 1952	Newcastle United	Hillsborough	0–0
22 March 1958	Bolton Wanderers	Maine Road	1–2
26 March 1960	Sheffield Wednesday	Maine Road	2–1

The club's two appearances in the Charity Shield *v.* Queen's Park Rangers (at White Hart Lane on 4 May 1912) and *v.* Everton (at Old Trafford on 24 October 1928) and Full Members' Cup final *v.* Charlton Athletic (at Wembley on 29 March 1987) also qualify, as do the club's numerous FA Cup finals at the Kennington Oval and Wembley.

Keith Newton

BORN IN MANCHESTER, Keith Newton started his football career by playing left-back for Didsbury Technical School at the age of eleven and continued to play for them until he was fifteen. After playing at right-back for Manchester Junior Boys, he played for Spurley Hey Youth Club when he was noticed by Blackburn Rovers.

He signed as professional in October 1958 and was a member of the successful Blackburn FA Youth Cup-winning side of 1959. Having appeared as a centre-half with the youth team, Newton made his first-team debut in the left-half position but switched to left-back, making the position his own.

Newton was a cultured defender. Tall and athletic, he was sharp in the tackle and sound in the air. He was also noted for his attacking runs down the flank. He finally settled into the right-back spot and won his first major honour in 1964, when he gained the first of several England Under-23 caps against Scotland at Newcastle. Shortly after this he

 Keith Newton: cool, cultured and vastly experienced full-back.

suffered the first of several major injuries that dogged his career and cost him many representative honours. He injured a knee training with England and had to have a cartilage operation. However, he subsequently made a remarkable recovery in time to go on England's close season Under-23 tour.

He got his first full cap in February 1965 at Wembley against West Germany, but it ended in near disaster. He was carried off the field with a suspected broken leg before the interval, but the injury turned out to be less serious than feared. Unfortunately, these injuries hampered his early career and he just missed out on inclusion in the 1966 World Cup. Despite the fact that Rovers were playing in the Second Division, Newton established himself as England's right-back in the late 1960s.

The Blackburn manager tried to persuade Newton that his future lay in mid-field and played him there on several occasions; but Newton was reluctant to switch positions on a permanent basis and reverted to his full-back role. By 1969 he was a world-rated player, though Rovers were continuing to struggle in Division Two, eventually finishing in the club's lowest-ever position to date.

In December 1969 he joined Everton for £80,000 and helped them to win the 1969–70 championship. After the initial success at Everton, Newton became more and more unsettled at the way he was being asked to play, and finally lost his place. In June 1972 he moved to Burnley on a free transfer, helping them win promotion to the First Division in the 1972–3 season. A cool, cultured and vastly experienced full-back, he remained at Turf Moor for the rest of his league career, before finally bowing out at the end of the 1977–8 season.

Nicknames

Many players in the club's history have been fondly known to supporters by their nicknames. One of the first was Albert Houlker (1896–1909). Popularly nicknamed 'Kelly' perhaps because, with his stocky build and black hair, he was an archetypal Irishman; he was capable of filling any of the three half-back positions, although he favoured the left side.

Known to all as 'Taffy', Herbert Jones (1925–33) was a cultured full-back signed from his home-town club Blackpool for the then considerable fee of £3,850.

Not the tallest of men ever to wear the Rovers' number five shirt, but Willie Kelly (1951–6) certainly lived up to his 'Iron Man' tag, for this rugged Scot's game was built on sheer physical aggression—as many renowned opponents would testify!

Ally MacLeod (1956–61) was John Carey's costliest signing when he joined Blackburn from St Mirren. Hugely popular, he was nick-named 'Noddy' by the Ewood crowd because of a peculiar nodding motion he made with his head when running.

Derek Dougan (1959–61) arrived from Portsmouth and quickly developed a rapport with the Blackburn public, who nicknamed him 'Cheyenne' after a popular television character. He revelled in his popu-larity and the younger Blackburn fans became fascinated by his antics.

Affectionately known as 'The Tank', John Bray (1959–65) was extremely popular with the supporters. A strong, barrel-chested full-back, he could play on either flank.

Rovers' commercial manager Ken Beamish (1974–6) was a firm favourite with the fans. The Ewood terraces rang to the chants of 'Beamo, Beamo'—a nickname which stuck for the rest of his career. In his present capacity, it was typical of the humour of the man to have 'Beamo' flash on the scoreboard when scoring opportunities were missed.

During the early days of his Ewood career Glenn Keeley (1976–87), who was to captain the side in the 1987 Full Members' Cup final, was prone to reckless challenges. these not only incurred the wrath of the referees but led to his being affectionately nicknamed 'Killer Keeley'.

Popularly known as 'Basil', Mick Rathbone (1979–87) came to Blackburn Rovers on a month's loan from Birmingham City. A former England Youth international, he went on to make over 300 first-team appearances before he moved to neighbours Preston in the summer of 1987.

Official Souvenir Programme £1

WELLING UTD

SEASON 1988-89

**V
BLACKBURN ROVERS
Saturday 7th January, 1989
Kick-Off 2.00 pm
F.A. Cup Third Round Proper**

SPONSORS

VAUXHALL
CONFERENCE

**Jackson
PROPERTY SERVICES**

HALIFAX
ESTATE AGENTS

*Programme cover for Rovers' match at Welling United, where a Ronnie
Hildersley goal settled the issue.*

Non-league

'NON-LEAGUE' is the shorthand term for clubs which are not members of the Football League. Blackburn have a very good record against non-league clubs in the FA Cup competition and have never lost a game, though on two occasions the Rovers needed a replay to win through.

The club's record is:

Date	Opponents	Venue	Score
24 November 1973	Willington	Away	0–0
3 December 1973	Willington	Home	6–1
15 December 1973	Altrincham	Home	0–0
19 December 1973	Altrincham	Away	2–0
23 November 1974	Matlock Town	Away	4–1
24 November 1979	Kidderminster Harriers	Away	2–0
17 December 1979	Stafford Rangers	Home	2–0
7 January 1989	Welling United	Away	1–0
4 January 1992	Kettering Town	Home	4–1

Official Inquiry

IN THE 1902–3 season Rovers avoided relegation by the skin of their teeth after taking seven points out of the last possible ten. The final relegation place had been between Rovers and Grimsby Town, with Bolton Wanderers already doomed. However, a month after the season ended it appeared that fate may well have been given a helping hand. There were rumours in the Grimsby area that two of Rovers' final games, against Bury (away 1–1) and Everton (away 3–0), had been arranged beforehand. An official inquiry was held and the following statement was issued:

We are of the opinion that J. Walmsley, the secretary of Blackburn Rovers Football Club, approached representatives of the Everton club and endeavoured to arrange that the Rovers should be allowed to win the match.

As a result of the inquiry Walmsley was suspended *sine die* from future football management and Everton were censured for not reporting the matter. Convinced that Walmsley had acted on his own, the inquiry took no further action against Blackburn Rovers.

Oozehead

THE ROVERS' first ground was a field at Oozehead, near to St Silas' School in Preston New Road. The venue was very rudimentary and had no facilities for either players or spectators. Almost in the middle of the field was a pond, which had to be covered with wooden planks and grass turf! The club had that ground for the 1876–7 season only.

Own Goals

THOUGH THERE HAVE been a number of instances of own goals over the years, it is Mick McGrath's own goal when Rovers played Wolves at Wembley in 1960 that is best remembered. McGrath was horizontal on the ground as Barry Stobart's cross evaded the diving Leyland. In attempting to find the safety of the dead-ball line, he toe-ended the ball and it flew into the net!

Penalties

AFTER Jim Forrest had converted the first one received in 1894, the Rovers missed the next three—this came at a time when the penalty

kick was a new experience and the commonly held perception was that there was not an earthly chance of a penalty kick being missed. Between 12 February 1927 and 21 February 1928 the club missed seven consecutive penalties—Harper (2), Hutton (2), Mitchell, Puddefoot and Healless were the guilty men. However, the side was clearly not over-dependent on penalties, as Rovers did win the FA Cup that season.

Jock McKay (1921–7) turned each penalty kick he took for Rovers into a separate piece of theatre. His jinks and feints often left the visitors' goalkeeper totally bewildered before he even kicked the ball.

Sometimes, though, it was the opposition goalkeeper that tried it on. As a Second Division club in 1952, Rovers had battled to the fifth round of the FA Cup where they were drawn to meet First Division West Bromwich Albion at Ewood on 23 February. With five minutes to go and the game goal-less, Rovers were awarded a penalty. It was a situation that needed a cool head, and in skipper Bill Eckersley Rovers had the man for the job. He was so calm that he was reported afterwards as having held a conversation with the Albion 'keeper as he put the ball on the spot ready to take the kick. When Heath, the Albion goalkeeper, came out Eckersley asked him what he wanted, to which the 'keeper replied, 'I'm seeing that the ball's on the spot.' As the story goes, Eckersley's quick-fire answer was, 'It'll soon be in the net.' And indeed it was.

Perhaps John Coddington's miss will always be remembered. He started his run ten yards outside the penalty area for a kick which barely arrived at the goalkeeper, was asked to re-take it because the goalkeeper had moved, and succeeded in adopting the same tactics with identical results!

The youngest penalty-taker the club has had is Peter Dobing who was aged 19 years 113 days when he took and scored with his first penalty kick.

Obviously, missed penalties are relative to the number of penalties actually taken, but Bryan Douglas holds the record with nine misses!

Fred Pickering

WHEN HE TURNED professional with Blackburn Rovers in 1958, Fred Pickering was being groomed as a full-back, but with the club so well served in that department his opportunities were limited. He had enjoyed success in the Rovers' junior teams, helping to win the FA Youth Cup in 1959, but when given a first-team chance he had failed to make a lasting impression. Rovers' manager Jack Marshall decided to gamble with him at centre-forward after some powerful displays in that position while playing with the reserves. Despite his initial clumsy approach work, Pickering had the happy knack of putting the ball in the net, and was soon to make quite a name for himself. He had begun to add pace and power to his game, and played havoc with the best defences in the land.

After 123 league game and fifty-nine goals in the Blackburn first team, he became unsettled and wanted a transfer. Blackburn were in their best league position for years but, incredibly and controversially, the club let him go. A fee of £85,000 took him to Everton where he was, at the time, the highest-priced player in a domestic transfer deal. It was to prove a wise signing, as the tall, dashing centre-forward threatened defences throughout the First Division. He began well by scoring a hat-trick on his home debut, yet it was in those final few games of the season that Everton lost the title—Pickering possibly upsetting the balance and rhythm of the side!

Fred Pickering is one of only four players this century who have achieved hat-tricks when making their debuts for England in full internationals—this he achieved against the USA in May 1964. The following season he proved to be worth every penny of his huge transfer fee as he collected twenty-seven goals. In March 1966 in the local derby with Liverpool he was completely on his own when he twisted and his leg collapsed under him. After missing a couple of games he returned, only for it to go again against Sheffield United when he went up for a high ball and came down on his knee. He had to miss the FA Cup semi-final and the final against Sheffield Wednesday. Popular with the Everton fans he could, with fewer injuries and a different temperament, have become one of the really great Everton footballers.

In August 1967 he moved to Birmingham City for £50,000 and proved to be a prolific marksman for the Midlands club with twenty-seven goals in seventy-four league appearances. He returned to Lancashire in 1969 when Blackpool paid £45,000 for him. After helping the Seasiders to win promotion to the First Division, he returned to Blackburn in March 1971.

Pickering was cast in the role of a saviour as Rovers faced Third Division football for the first time in their history. Early in 1971–2 Rovers' boss Ken Furphy allowed him to be released, claiming he was out of condition. He attempted to revive his career with Brighton, but without success. Though he made his mark with Everton, he will always be remembered by Blackburn fans as the player who could have led the club to championship success.

Plastic

THERE HAVE BEEN four Football League clubs that have replaced their normal grass playing pitches with artificial surfaces at one stage or another. Queen's Park Rangers were the first in 1981, but the Loftus Road plastic was discarded in 1988 in favour of a return to turf. Luton Town (1985), Oldham Athletic (1986) and Preston North End (1986) followed.

The Rovers have never played on the Kenilworth Road or Deepdale plastic. They visited the Loftus Road plastic on two occasions, losing 0–2 in 1981–2 and drawing 2–2 the following the season. The club has been a regular visitor to Boundary Park, and though the Rovers' record on their plastic pitch is not a good one, it is probably no worse than that of most clubs.

Rovers' results on the Boundary Park plastic (all in the Second Division):

1986–7	Lost	0–3
1987–8	Lost	2–4
1988–9	Drew	1–1
1989–90	Lost	0–2
1990–1	Drew	1–1

Player of the Year

THIS AWARD by Blackburn supporters dates from season 1969–70 and the winners have been as follows:

1969–70	Ken Knighton	1981–2	
1970–71	Roger Jones	1982–3	Simon Garner
1971–2	John McNamee	1983–4	
1972–3	Tony Field	1984–5	Terry Gennoe
1973–4	Derek Fazackerley	1985–6	Simon Barker
1974–5	Don Martin	1986–7	David Mail
1975–6	Tony Parkes	1987–8	Colin Hendry
1976–7		1988–9	Howard Gayle
1977–8	John Bailey	1989–90	Scott Sellars
1978–9	Derek Fazackerly	1990–91	Kevin Moran
1979–80	Glen Keeley	1991–2	Alan Wright
1980–1	Howard Kandall	1992–3	Colin Hendry

Play-offs

WHEN BLACKBURN triumphed against Leicester City at Wembley in the Division Two play-off final on 25 May 1992, it was fourth time lucky as far as the play-offs were concerned. For three successive seasons the Rovers suffered the heartbreak of reaching the play-offs but failed to emerge winners. In 1987–8 they were eliminated at the first hurdle by Chelsea. The following season saw a tense two-match battle against Watford as Rovers progressed to the final on the 'away goals' rule. After the team had defeated Crystal Palace 3–1 at Ewood, many thought the second leg at Selhurst Park a formality, but a crashing 3–0 defeat shattered the dream once more.

*A selection of programme covers from Rovers' exploits in the play-offs.
Above: Chelsea, 1–4. Opposite: Watford, 1–1. Following page: Crystal
Palace, 3–1.*

OFFICIAL MATCH PROGRAMME

The ROVERS

70p

BLACKBURN ROVERS · F.C.

18   75

ARTE ET LABORE

Blackburn Rovers   v Crystal Palace
Div. Two Play Off Final
Wednesday, May 31, 1989
Kick-off 7.45pm

BARCLAYS LEAGUE

TODAY'S MATCH SPONSORS
ICI Chemicals
and Polymers Ltd.,
Darwen.

A third appearance in successive seasons was guaranteed when Rovers scrambled a draw at home to Brighton in the last game of the season. However, an inept performance in the first leg of the semi-final against Swindon Town saw Rovers go down 2–1 at Ewood. Three days later Rovers were again defeated 2–1 as defensive errors cost them the

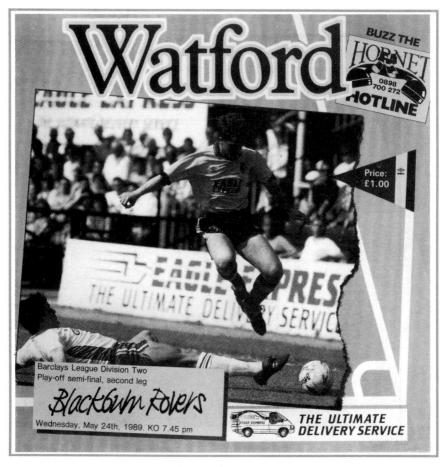

tie. Fortunately, it all came right at the fourth attempt, when a Mike Newell penalty was enough to beat Leicester City.

Points

UNDER THE three-points-for-a-win system which was introduced in 1981–2, the Rovers' *best points tally* is the seventy-seven points gained

in seasons 1987–8 and 1988–9 when the club finished fifth in the Second Division and was involved in the play-offs.

The club's *best points haul* under the old two-points-for-a-win system was sixty points from forty-six matches in 1974–5, which would have netted the club eighty-two points under the present method.

The *worst* record under either system was the meagre twenty points secured in 1965–6 when the club was relegated to the Second Division.

Postponed

AFTER A SUDDEN downpour at 2.30 p.m. on the afternoon of Rovers' last match of the 1985–6 season against Grimsby Town, the match was postponed. At the time it appeared as if this postponement was of a rather tactical nature, given the lowly position of Rovers. The game was replayed on the Monday night when Rovers, needing to win to stay in the Second Division and inspired by the incisive Simon Garner, stormed home to a 3–1 victory.

Premier League

THE FIRST SEASON of Premier League soccer contained so much worth remembering for Blackburn's fans as the Rovers claimed their highest position in English football for seventy-eight years.

Of course there was the occasional hiccup. No-one could disguise the disappointment of going out of the two cup competitions with Wembley so close, while in the league there were a couple of silly scorelines—5–2 defeats at home to Coventry City and away to Leeds United.

In the first few weeks of the season Rovers enjoyed a run of five 'clean sheets' in six games, while £3.3m striker Alan Shearer was in sensational form. There are many who believe that if Blackburn had not been shorn of Shearer's services there would now be a trophy standing on the Ewood sideboard.

The season surpassed all expectations as Rovers finished in fourth place in the inaugural Premier League. The season's record was:

P	W	D	L	F	A	Pts
42	20	11	11	68	46	71

Preston North End

ROVERS' MEETINGS with North End have always been something special; the highlight of the season's calender, dating back even before the formation of the Football League in 1888. In the old days it was not unknown for the keener fans to walk to an away game, ten miles either way. It is on record that in 1881 (seven years before football's first ever league competition) the Rovers beat North End 16–0 in a friendly match at Preston!

In the first season of the league it was North End who made history by winning the championship without losing a single game. They also, that same season, won the FA Cup without conceding a goal. The meeting in Blackburn, which was before Ewood Park was opened (the game was at the old Leamington ground) ended in a 2–2 draw.

One curious fact in the list of results is that, in a sequence of ten consecutive meetings at Ewood between 1920 and 1949, Preston had nine wins! The exception was Christmas 1921, when Ewood Park's all-time record crowd for a league match—52,656—packed the stands and terraces to see Rovers triumph 3–0.

Since the days of the historic Old Invincibles, many great players and colourful characters have shared in some tremendous tussles. Bob Crompton used to revel in those derby days in the so-called golden age before the First World War. In the 1913–14 First Division championship run, when he was captain, the Rovers had their biggest league win of the series 5–0. Afterwards, North End had such stars as Alex James and, in a later era, Tom Finney, the two Beatties, and many others. Finney put on a superlative display in October 1959, inspiring a 4–1 Preston win. This was one of the three occasions in post-war football that Rovers–North End games at Ewood Park drew 40,000-plus attendances.

There have been some interesting transfer links between the clubs, too. It was from Ewood to Deepdale that Bobby Langton first moved in 1948 (returning by way of Bolton five years later), and it was from Deepdale that Eddie Quigley came to save the Rovers in the classic revival of 1951–2.

There have been two other occasions when Preston North End appeared at Ewood and the Rovers didn't. One was the second of the wartime cup finals in 1941 when they met Arsenal in a replay after a Wembley draw; the other an FA Cup second-round replay against Bolton Wanderers which drew a full house, and a fabulous goal by Nat Lofthouse beat them.

Promotion

THE ROVERS have won promotion five times. Having suffered relegation for the first time in 1935–6, the Ewood Park club set about ensuring its return to the top flight with the minimum of delay, but it took three seasons to achieve this aim. Winning twenty-five of its matches, the club established a new record for the number of victories in a season as it headed the Second Division of 1938–9.

P	W	D	L	F	A	Pts
42	25	5	12	94	60	55

Then came the war, but, after only two seasons in the First Division, the club was relegated once more. This time it took Rovers ten seasons to win their way back again, finishing as runners-up to West Ham United in 1957–8.

P	W	D	L	F	A	Pts
42	22	12	8	93	57	56

After another relegation in 1966 the Rovers spent five seasons in Division Two before relegation to the Third Division for the first time in the club's history. After four seasons the Rovers were promoted in

 The Blackburn side that finished as runners-up to West Ham in 1957–8.

1974–5 as Third Division champions, securing sixty points, the club's highest under the two-points-for-a-win system.

P	W	D	L	F	A	Pts
42	22	16	8	68	45	60

Unfortunately, four seasons later the Rovers were back in the Third Division, but won immediate promotion in 1979–80 as they finished runners-up to Grimsby Town. After a poor start to the campaign the side, under Howard Kendall, embarked on a long unbeaten run which included a sequence of fourteen wins out of fifteen league matches.

P	W	D	L	F	A	Pts
46	25	9	12	58	36	59

After twelve seasons in the Second Division, and many close calls, including reaching the play-offs on four occasions, the Rovers won through to what was to become the Premier League after beating

Leicester City 1–0 at Wembley; where Mike Newell scored the all-important goal from the penalty spot. Blackburn had finished in sixth place in Division Two with the following record:

P	W	D	L	F	A	Pts
46	21	11	14	70	53	74

Though there may be other changes in the years ahead, there won't be too many clubs who will go straight to the Premier League from the Second Division!

Eddie Quigley

IN DECEMBER 1949 Eddie Quigley became the most expensive foot-baller in Britain when he joined Preston North End from Sheffield Wednesday for £26,000.

As a player, his movements were totally deceptive, for his speed of thought and precise passing made him a constant threat to the opposition defences. He was capable of playing both inside- or cen-tre-forward, though he preferred to play much deeper than most of his contemporaries. Under Johnny Carey's attacking philosophy, Quigley's goal-scoring flourished, his long-range shooting having both accuracy and power.

On leaving Ewood in August 1956, he returned to his home-town club, Bury, for a short spell before entering non-league football to manage Mossley. After returning to Gigg Lane as coach, he managed Stockport County before joining Rovers as assistant manager in November 1966.

Although only assistant manager, Eddie Quigley had insisted that he be in sole charge of coaching throughout the club. A master tactician, he soon began to show his influence on Jack Marshall's team. Following Marshall's resignation in February 1967, Quigley was ap-pointed caretaker manager, a position that became permanent some two months later. Though he kept Rovers in the promotion hunt for the next two seasons, the club didn't mount a serious challenge.

In October 1970, with the club languishing at the foot of the Second Division, it was agreed that Quigley and administrative manager Johnny Carey exchange duties. Though he was put in charge of scouting and looking after Rovers' youngsters, he, along with Carey, was sacked following the club's relegation to the Third Division.

He found employment with Rovers a third time in 1979 when Howard Kendall appointed him chief scout, a position he held until Kendall left in 1981, thus ending an association which, on and off, had lasted almost thirty years.

Rapid Scoring

SIGNED FROM Sheffield Wednesday, John McIntyre scored four goals in five minutes for Blackburn Rovers against Everton at Ewood Park on 16 September 1922, and all of them were at the Darwen end. The Rovers won 5–1.

The first half had been extremely disappointing for the Ewood crowd and, though Rovers had been on top, as so often happens Everton scored against the run of play. On the stroke of half time, as the home crowd were beginning to get restless, Healless equalised with a long-range effort. In the second half, McIntyre wrote his name into the club's record books. He served notice of his intentions with a fierce volley which flew just outside the woodwork. After eleven minutes of the second half he put Rovers ahead, and before the visitors had time to regain their composure McIntyre struck twice more. Only two minutes after completing his hat-trick he fastened onto a Hodkinson centre and blasted his fourth goal in only five minutes.

Relegation

THE ROVERS have, on five occasions, experienced the anguish of relegation. The first came in 1936, but after only three seasons in the Second Division the club was back in Division One. Then came the

war and only two seasons of top-flight football before Rovers were back in Division Two.

Returning to the First Division at the end of the 1957–8 season, the Rovers were relegated in 1966, a prelude to the club's longest ever period of exile from First Division football. In 1971 the Rovers were relegated to the Third Division for the first time in their history, and, though the club returned to the Second Division in 1975, four seasons later they were back in the Third. Twelve months later Rovers were promoted, and after twelve seasons of Second Division football now play in the Premier League.

'Round Robin'

ON MONDAY 16 February 1931 it was made public that there was disagreement at Ewood Park with the manager of Rovers. Since Jack Carr had resigned, Bob Crompton had acted in an honorary capacity and had taken charge of the training and management of the team. It was then that the difficulties arose.

A week before the news became public property, the players signed a 'Round Robin' in which they called attention to certain alleged grievances they had. It was handed to the chairman, J. W. Walsh, who immediately made Crompton aware of the contents of the document. He voluntarily decided to avoid any friction and discontinued his duties for the time being.

In March the club held its annual meeting amidst newspaper reports which suggested that more than one player had come to regret the way in which events had developed. The meeting had to elect five directors, but Bob Crompton failed to gain re-election.

In Crompton's absence the Rovers were relegated to the Second Division for the first time in their history. The public in general wanted Bob Crompton to be recalled, and in March 1938 the directors bowed to the inevitable and approached him. So on 2 April 1938 Crompton took over, and under his guidance Blackburn managed to avoid relegation. Promotion to the First Division followed in 1938–9, as Crompton began to build a team to restore the club's fortunes.

'Rovers Cottage'

IN 1886, when things were not going too well, the Rovers had a big prize draw. Thousands of tickets were sold at 6d. each, and the first prize was the 'Rovers Cottage', valued at £140. A picture of it appeared on the sweep ticket, and its description:

> The cottage is newly built, palisaded in front and situated on New Bank Road, near the Rovers' Football Ground, Blackburn. The land is freehold (subject to a yearly ground rent of One Pound fifteen Shillings) and will entitle the winner to a county vote.

One ticket had six purchasers. Five of them put their pennies down readily, but the sixth had to be persuaded to risk a copper. Eventually he did so. The half-dozen men raffled the ticket among themselves and it was won by the reluctant one. Attending the draw on Wednesday 17 March 1886, he discovered that it was his ticket that bore the winning number!

Rovers' Return

ON 5 FEBRUARY 1955 Tommy Briggs scored seven goals in a row, including one penalty for Blackburn Rovers in an 8–3 win over Bristol Rovers. Yet on 6 November 1954 he had failed to score in Rovers' record 9–0 success over Middlesbrough!

Bob Saxton

BOB SAXTON joined Rovers from Plymouth Argyle in the summer of 1981 as the club reverted to its old formula of choosing a man with a proven track-record from the lower divisions.

He immediately reorganised the back-room staff, bringing in Jim Furnell, Harold Jarman and Tony Long with him, whilst appointing Tony Parkes as coach. He strengthened the playing squad with two signings of players who were to give distinguished service to Rovers— Terry Gennoe and Ian Miller. After three years of consolidating the club's position in the Second Division, Saxton was able to mount a serious promotion challenge in 1984–5, as newly-signed Jimmy Quinn gave the club variety in attack. At Christmas the Rovers headed the table, but in the New Year the team inexplicably began to falter. Saxton refused to sign new players, believing that the squad who had taken Rovers to the top of the table should be given the chance to complete the job. This failure to win promotion from such a strong position led to unrest on the terraces.

The following season saw the Rovers escape relegation in the very last match of the season, when they beat Grimsby 3–1. By Christmas of the 1986–7 season the club had made little improvement, and were rooted to the foot of the table. The fans called for the manager's head, and, though initially both the chairman and the players tried to clear Saxton of blame, the board finally bowed to the growing pressure and he was sacked.

Second Division

BLACKBURN ROVERS have had five separate spells in the Second Division. When the club was relegated at the end of the 1935–6 season the directors took charge of team affairs, but their attempt at team management saw the club struggling at the wrong end of the division for two seasons. In April 1938 Bob Crompton returned, lifted the team, and relegation was avoided. The legend of Bob Crompton soared to new heights when, in 1938–9, he took the club to the Second Division championship.

Following Bob Crompton's death in March 1941, the club resumed after the war with Eddie Hapgood, the former Arsenal and England full-back, in charge. After a few months it was clear that a relegation battle was all the season had to offer. The opening weeks of 1947 saw a rift between Hapgood and the board develop over the purchase of

new players, and in February he resigned. Having narrowly avoided relegation, the Rovers began the 1947–8 campaign under Will Scott's managership. Dogged by illness, he was forced to resign and was replaced by Jack Bruton. Despite some disappointing results, Bruton began to rebuild the team, though relegation did take on an air of inevitability. The club spent the next ten seasons in the Second Division before finishing as runners-up to West Ham United in 1957–8, beating Charlton 4–3 in the final game of the season. The 1954–5 campaign had seen Rovers score 114 goals, including a 9–0 beating of Middlesbrough, while Tommy Briggs scored seven goals in the 8–3 defeat of Bristol Rovers.

Eight seasons in the First Division followed, before a disappointing season in 1965–6 resulted in Rovers returning to the Second Division for a third spell. Unfortunately, things went from bad to worse and in 1970–1 the club was relegated to the Third Division for the first time in its history. Only four seasons were needed before the Rovers won the championship in 1974–5 to return to the Second Division.

Under the leadership of Jim Smith the club survived a difficult first season back in the Second Division, but by 1977–8 Smith had assembled a squad of players good enough to be involved in the promotion battle. However, in March 1977 he left to join Birmingham City, and was replaced by Jim Iley. After he had spent only 172 days in charge, the board terminated his contract, and, though John Pickering was promoted from coach to the manager's office, the club was relegated to the third Division at the end of the 1978–9 season. After appointing Howard Kendall as its first player-manager, the club bounced back immediately, finishing as runners-up. There then followed twelve seasons in the Second Division—the club's longest period in this standard—before promotion to the newly formed Premier League in 1991–2. There were many occasions when the club was in contention for promotion, and on four occasions was involved in the play-offs. It was the play-offs that resulted in Rovers leaving the Second Division when they beat Leicester City 1–0 at Wembley.

Blackburn's all-time record in Division Two is:

P	W	D	L	F	A
1446	583	364	499	2148	1994

 Programme cover for the third-round match at Ipswich in the Simod Cup, Rovers' very last game in this competition.

Silver Shield

IN RECOGNITION of Rovers' third consecutive victory in the FA Cup final of 1886, the Football Association presented the club with a beautiful silver shield.

In the upper portion is a representation of the cup, surmounted by a miniature football and a plate bearing the words 'Blackburn Rovers Football Club 1886'. In the centre of the shield is a plate with the inscription 'Presented by the Football Association in commemoration of their winning the Challenge Cup three years in succession, viz 1884, 1885 and 1886, April 3rd 1886 at Kennington Oval, beat West Bromwich Albion by two goals to none.' Underneath are two oval-shaped plates inscribed '1884, Kennington Oval, beat Queen's Park, Glasgow two goals to one', and '1885, Kennington Oval, beat Queen's Park, Glasgow, two goals to love'.

Simod Cup

THE SIMOD CUP replaced the Full Members' Cup for the 1987–8 season. The Rovers' first-round match that season saw them go down 1–2 at home to Swindon Town, with Nicky Reid scoring the Blackburn goal. The following season saw the club reach the third round after victories over Manchester City (home 3–1 after extra time) and Sunderland (home 2–1). Rovers went out to the only goal of the game at Portman Road, Ipswich on 10 January 1989, the club's last game in this competition.

Jim Smith

A TYPICALLY TOUGH Yorkshireman, Jim Smith played with Sheffield United, Aldershot, Halifax Town and Lincoln City before becoming

player-manager at non-league Boston United. His success here led to his being appointed manager of Colchester United in 1972, where he immediately rewarded their faith in him by winning promotion for the team to the Third Division.

When Jim Smith arrived at Ewood in the summer of 1975, he inherited a winning team and a crowd with high expectations of continued success. However, the team began to struggle, and it was only after the signings of veteran wingers Dave Wagstaffe and Gordon Taylor that Rovers improved and thus retained their newly-won Second Division status.

Smith now began to build a Blackburn side which reflected his approach to the game. His team was capable of playing the most exciting attacking football, but it was also unpredictable and lost matches which, on paper, should have been won. As a result, despite being well-placed, promotion always looked out of reach and the team ended the season in fifth place.

As the promotion flame of this 1977–8 campaign began to die, Jim Smith accepted the managership of Birmingham City, and within a matter of weeks had taken Norman Bodell, his assistant, with him.

He enjoyed mixed fortunes at St Andrews before moving to Oxford United. Here he had his most successful period as a manager, taking the unfashionable club from Third to First Division before he moved to Loftus Road to manager Queen's Park Rangers.

In 1988 he accepted the challenge to manage Newcastle United, and, although the Magpies were relegated, Jim Smith did at least restore some pride on Tyneside. Now manager at Portsmouth, he has led Pompey to an FA Cup semi-final and the play-offs in the last two seasons.

Snowstorm

ON 12 DECEMBER 1891 Herbie Arthur, the Rovers' goalkeeper, had a peculiar experience in the game at Burnley. During a memorable blizzard, the rest of the Blackburn side had left the field, half-frozen and blinded with the sleet—but Arthur stayed on to hold the fort against the whole Burnley team. A lot of ludicrous stories of what

Herbie Arthur: Rovers'
goalkeeper who stayed on to
hold the fort against the
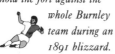 *whole Burnley*
team during an
1891 blizzard.

happened were circulated, but when the referee ordered the game to proceed and Burnley kicked-off, Arthur at once claimed off-side. The referee allowed the appeal, but Arthur hesitated so long in taking the free kick that the official wisely declared the game at an end!

Southport

SOUTHPORT's league career lasted from 1921–2, when they were founder members of the Third Division (North), until they failed to gain re-election in 1977–8, when they lost their place to Wigan Athletic on a second ballot.

Rovers first met Southport in the first round of the FA Cup in that 1921–2 season. Held at Ewood 1–1, the Rovers won the replay 2–1 with all their goals scored by Norman Rodgers. The two clubs met again in the third round of the FA Cup in 1926–7 when Southport

gained revenge with a 2–0 home win—their only success over the Rovers in seven meetings.

Fourth Division champions in 1972–3, the two clubs met on four occasions the following season. The teams were drawn together in the League Cup, and Rovers needed a Tony Field penalty before taking Southport to Ewood Park for a replay. Even then extra time was needed before Rovers ran out winners 3–1. There were similar results in the league as Blackburn drew 2–2 at Haig Avenue and won the home fixture 2–1.

Sponsors

THE FIRST NAME ever to be featured on the famous blue and white shirts was ICI Perspex, who first became involved for the televised FA Cup tie against Southampton in February 1984 and followed that up with a deal which lasted until June 1991.

On 6 June 1991 Rovers signed a new three-year sponsorship deal with Matthew Brown, worth in excess of £200,000. Carrying on their shirts the name 'McEwan's Lager'—a product of Matthew Brown's parent company, Scottish and Newcastle Breweries—the club was absolutely delighted not only to have got a national name, but that it preserved a local link through Matthew Brown. For its part, the brewery, too, was pleased to secure the sponsorship because as a Blackburn-based company, it knew how much Rovers means to local people.

Sports

THE ANNUAL Blackburn Rovers' Sports was a brave attempt by the directors to publicise the club and raise money at the same time by sponsoring athletic and cycling events. The prizemoney in 1892 was a staggering £130, which attracted no fewer than 400 competitors, among them Vogt, the Scottish cycling champion; Blair of Glasgow and Lavelle of Dublin (first and second in the furling), and Winder-

mere's Rawlinson, winner of the quarter-mile. The presence of the athletes from the Lake District denoted the promotion's importance in so far as it induced them to leave their highly competitive and rewarding local circuit. It would have been fitting if Rovers' own entry, Jimmy Southworth, could have won the furlong, but, although he qualified for the final, he finished unplaced.

Substitutes

SUBSTITUTES WERE first allowed in the Football League in the 1965–6 season. The first appearance of a substitute in league football came just down the road at Burnden Park, when Charlton Athletic's Keith Peacock came on during Wanderers' 4–2 win.

Blackburn's first substitute was John Byrom, who came on for Mick McGrath in the club's fifteenth game of the season; a 2–2 draw against Manchester United at Old Trafford. The team only had to wait until the following game for its first goal-scoring number twelve—John Byrom scoring in the 4–2 home win over Newcastle United.

The greatest number of substitutes used in a single season by the Rovers under the single-substitute rule was thirty in seasons 1972–

John Byrom: Blackburn's first goal-scoring substitute.

3 and 1976–7, but since 1986–7 two substitutes have been allowed, and in 1991–2 the club used seventy in forty-six matches.

The greatest number of substitute appearances for the Rovers has been made by Simon Garner, who had come on during twenty-nine league games before his move to West Bromwich Albion. It was in 1990–1 that Lenny Johnrose cause the Rovers' records on the matter of substitutes to be rewritten, with an extraordinary seventeen league appearances in the number twelve shirt.

Sunday Football

THE FIRST EVER Sunday matches in the Football League took place on 20 January 1974 during the three-day week imposed by the government during its trial of strength with the coalminers. The Rovers had to wait until the following Sunday, 27 January, before playing their first game on the Sabbath, defeating Shrewsbury Town 2–0 in front of 10,989—the club's biggest crowd of the season! In the club's other Sunday League matches that season they beat Southport 2–1 and drew 0–0 with Tranmere Rovers.

The club's next Sunday game was the Full Members' Cup final against Charlton Athletic on 29 March 1987, when Colin Hendry's goal was enough to give the team victory.

When Chelsea visited Ewood in the 1987–8 play-offs, it was Sunday 15 May; the following season Watford visited the Rovers on Sunday 21 May, and Rovers visited Selhurst Park on Sunday 4 June. In all of these games, Blackburn failed to score! The club's first goal in a Sunday play-off match came on 13 May 1990, when they went down 1–2 at home to Swindon Town.

In 1991–2 Rovers beat Derby County 4–2 on Sunday 10 May to give them the lead they needed to take them through to the Wembley play-off final on Monday 25 May 1992.

Suspensions

WHEN Joe Lofthouse was dismissed in the match against Burnley on 12 December 1891 he was suspended until 29 February 1892. However, on his return to the side he scored the winning goal in Rovers' 4–3 home win over Aston Villa.

Perhaps the strangest suspension of a Rovers player came in 1897, when George Anderson was suspended for 'failing to keep himself in shape'—but then the team got into relegation trouble and had to reinstate him!

Sustained Scoring

IN 1890–1 Jack Southworth scored twenty-six goals in his eighteen appearances, including four hat-tricks. He missed the last four games of the season, when the club scored only one goal!

The 1925–6 season belonged to Ted Harper. After scoring eighteen goals during the previous campaign—a post-war record—he made a re-appearance in the fourth game at Newcastle. He put five goals past the Magpies' goalkeeper, Wilson, who was on trial from Peeble Rovers, and in the next six games hit another nine goals, including a hat-trick, in the 6–3 defeat of Cardiff. By Christmas he had scored twenty-three goals, and by the end of the season forty-three. It was a First Division record, and would have been a league record but for the fact that Cookson of Chesterfield totalled forty-four in the same season in the Third Division (North).

Television

THE FIRST Rovers match to receive coverage on television was the Charlton Athletic–Rovers fifth-round FA Cup tie on 8 March 1947.

This was the first FA Cup tie other than the final to be televised—unfortunately, Rovers went down 0–1.

The club has also appeared on numerous occasions on both BBC and ITV, while the play-off final victory over Leicester on 25 May 1992 was shown 'live'. In 1992–3 Rovers featured seven times on Sky TV, bringing in almost £500,000. The first was a goal-less draw at Villa Park, while the first at Ewood was a 2–0 victory over Chelsea. The club also received £7,755 for each of the two main matches on BBC's *Match of the Day*, plus a limited number of midweek matches. In addition, the Rovers featured in the semi-finals of the Coca Cola Cup, both matches being shown 'live' by ITV.

'Test Matches'

WHEN THE 1897–8 season ended, the bottom of the First Division table read:

	P	W	D	L	F	A	Pts
Blackburn Rovers	30	7	10	13	39	54	24
Stoke City	30	8	8	14	35	55	24

In those days it was customary for the bottom two clubs of the First Division and the top two of the Second Division to play 'test matches' to decide which two should be numbered among the sixteen clubs of the First Division. There was no automatic promotion and relegation as we know it today.

In April 1898 the Rovers' results were:

v. Burnley	Home	Lost	1–3
v. Burnley	Away	Lost	0–2
v. Newcastle United	Home	Won	4–3
v. Newcastle United	Away	Lost	0–4

It looked like 'curtains' for the Rovers, as they finished bottom of that group of four. But Burnley proposed that the First and Second Division should each be extended to admit more clubs. The then Woolwich Arsenal and Aston Villa also proposed a re-arrangement of the clubs, but Burnley's scheme carried. The Rovers were elected by twenty-seven votes, and the 'test matches' abolished.

Third Division

THE ROVERS were relegated to the Third Division for the first time in their history at the end of the 1970–1 season.

The club's first game in the Third Division saw Rotherham United defeated 2–1 at Ewood Park on 14 August 1971 under new manager Ken Furphy. A mid-table position at the end of the season was followed by an unsuccessful promotion push in 1972–3. Strangely, it was during this season that the Football League ordered one of Rovers' matches to be replayed. A home defeat at the hands of Chesterfield was wiped out when it was discovered that their goalkeeper was not properly registered at the time of the match. The Rovers saw precious promotion points slip out of their grasp when Chesterfield returned to Ewood and again proved victorious. In 1974–5, under new manager Gordon Lee, the club stormed to the top of the table and remained there for most of the season, to gain promotion.

After four fairly difficult seasons the club was relegated to the Third Division for a second time, and appointed Howard Kendall as its first player-manager. After a poor start to the 1979–80 season, Kendall's side embarked on a long unbeaten run which included fourteen wins out of fifteen matches and achieved promotion at the first time of asking. The club's last game in the Third Division was a 1–2 reversal at home to Bury!

Rovers' full playing record in the Third Division is as follows:

P	W	D	L	F	A	Pts
230	104	59	67	299	249	267

 Mike Newell: Blackburn Rovers' first £1 million player, seen here with Manager, Kenny Dalglish.

Transfers

THE TRANSFER of players has always been a feature of football, though in the early days some unusual arrangements were made.

Tom Brandon, who won an FA Cup-winners' medal in 1891, was enticed across the Pennines to join Sheffield Wednesday with both a favourable contract and the promise of a public house!

In January 1911 Rovers paid Falkirk a record transfer fee of £1,800 for Jock Simpson, while two years later £2,000 bought Danny Shea from Southern League West Ham, his twenty-seven goals going a long way to ensuring that the League Championship came to Ewood at the end of the 1913–14 season.

When Rovers paid neighbours Burnley £6,500 for Jack Bruton in December 1929 it was the most that the Ewood Park club had paid for a player. The club paid their first five-figure fee for a player on 30

January 1947 when they signed Jock Weir, Hibernian's centre-forward, reputedly for a fee of £10,000.

When Fred Pickering joined Everton in March 1964 for £85,000 it was, at the time, a British record fee. Other players to command record fees were Duncan McKenzie, who joined Rovers from Chelsea in March 1979 for £80,000, and Simon Barker, Rovers receiving £400,000 from Queen's Park Rangers in July 1988.

Colin Hendry joined Rovers from Dundee for £30,000 in March 1987, and then left to join Manchester City for £700,000 in November 1989 before returning to Ewood two years later for the same fee.

The club's first million-pound player was Mike Newell, who joined Rovers from Everton in November 1991 for £1.1 million, while in the summer of 1992 Alan Shearer became Rovers' most expensive player ever, when he signed from Southampton for £3.6 million.

Trawlers

SOME OF THE FINEST of Grimsby trawlers were named after football teams. The *Blackburn Rovers* made her first appearance in 1934 and shortly afterwards set out on a fishing expedition to Iceland, where she made a magnificent catch which sold for £1,800.

Undefeated

BLACKBURN ROVERS have remained undefeated at home throughout four league seasons: 1888–9 (the first season of the Football League); 1909–10; 1911–12 and 1933–4.

The club's best and longest undefeated home sequence in the Football League is of thirty matches between 8 April 1911 and 21 December 1912.

The Rovers' longest run of undefeated Football League matches, *home and away*, is twenty-three between 30 September 1987 and 5 March 1988.

Unusual Goals

THERE HAVE BEEN a number of unusual goals scored at Ewood Park over the years. One of the most unusual goals of all time was scored by Edward Bracegirdle, a fleet-footed little winger who was also a professional sprinter. Albert Iremonger, Notts County's 6 ft. 5 ins. goalkeeper, was entrusted with a penalty kick, but struck the crossbar. The rebound went to Bracegirdle who hared off for the other goal, pursued only by Iremonger. The winger won the race quite comfortably and tapped the ball into the empty net.

More of an unusual incident, but still resulting in a goal, occurred in the match against Arsenal at Ewood Park on Christmas Day 1928. The Gunners were a goal in front when they were penalised as goalkeeper Lewis carried the ball too far. The free kick was awarded only five yards from the goal line and the referee warned the Arsenal team that they could either stand behind the goal line or behind the person taking the kick. At the instigation of David Jack, who obviously believed that in doing so they would play the recipient of the ball off-side, they stood ten yards behind. Naturally, Healless tapped the indirect free kick to one side and Puddefoot walked the ball home!

Utility Players

A UTILITY PLAYER is one of those particularly gifted footballers who can play in several, or even many, different positions. Probably the earliest utility player at the Rovers was Hugh McIntyre who, between 1880 and 1886, occupied full-back, wing-half and centre-forward positions. He even kept goal in the Lancashire Cup Final of 1885–6 when Rovers lost by the only goal to Preston North End.

Sam McClure was another exceptionally talented Rovers player who, though he settled down at centre-half, was a more than useful wing-half and centre-forward. He had signed for Everton as a goalkeeper and did make one appearance for the Rovers in this position in the 3–3 draw with Sheffield United on 13 April 1900.

Harry Healless, the man who held the FA Cup aloft in 1928, was capable of filling any of the half-back positions, even though his initial first-team appearances were in the forward line.

After about the mid-1960s players were encouraged to become more adaptable and to see their roles as less stereotyped. At the same time, however, much less attention came to be paid to the implication of wearing a certain numbered shirt and, accordingly, some of the more versatile players came to wear almost all the different numbered shirts at some stage or another, although this did not necessarily indicate a vast variety of positions. Paul Round, who made sixty first-team appearances for Blackburn between 1977 and 1981, wore ever outfield shirt except number eleven.

Victories

In a season

THE ROVERS' greatest number of victories in a season is twenty-five in 1938–9, which included seventeen at home—another record.

In a match

Rovers' best victories in the major competitions are as follows:

Home

Football League	9–0	*v.* Middlesbrough	1954–5
FA Cup	8–1	*v.* Aston Villa	1888–9
Football League Cup	6–1	*v.* Watford	1992–3

Away

Football League	8–2	*v.* West Ham United	1963–4
FA Cup	7–0	*v.* Bootle	1889–90
Football League Cup	5–1	*v.* Bolton Wanderers	1964–5

These results are for matches played since the club's admission to the Football League, though prior to that Rovers beat Rossendale 11–0 at home on 13 October 1884 in the first round of the FA Cup.

Jack Walker

ACCORDING TO a national newspaper, Blackburn Rovers is a back-street football club! Just as well, then, that Jack Walker—probably the most popular man in Blackburn, and one of Britain's twenty-five wealthiest men—knows a thing or two about back streets.

The Jack Walker story starts in 1945, in the Blackburn back streets, almost within sight of Ewood Park's floodlit towers. The war had just ended when Jack Walker joined his dad, Charles, who, with £80, had started a tiny sheet metal working and car body repair business among the cobbles. In 1950 Jack was called up for National Service in the army. The following year Mr Charles Walker died, and Jack, who returned to the business, built up with brother Fred a turnover of £80,000 by 1956. That was the year that the Walkers entered the steel stockholding business, putting into motion one of East Lancashire's most remarkable success stories. For by 1989 the £80-business was an empire with sales of £623m and 3,400 employees in sixty locations throughout the United Kingdom and Ireland. Then in October 1989 the Walkers sold out to British Steel—the £330m price made the deal the United Kingdom's biggest ever private sale. By May 1990 the sale had cleared the regulatory authorities and gone through, and Jack Walker could look for another interest.

Having retired to his home in Mount Cochon, Jersey in the '70s, Jack Walker never forgot his roots—for the Blackburn-born, Blackburn-bred and Blackburn-made man chose Rovers.

So it was that when Jack Walker arrived at Ewood he invited 'King' Kenny Dalglish to manage the team. And the rest is news.

There's only one Jack Walker!

 Jack Walker, probably the most popular man in Blackburn!

War Cup Final

WHEN THE CLUB'S record in knockout competitions is discussed, this is a Wembley appearance that is rarely mentioned. It came in June 1940 when Rovers met West Ham United in the League War Cup final and the Londoners won 1–0. A restricted attendance of 43,000 turned up at Wembley to see the winners of the north and south semi-finals, and the spectators included a section of Dunkirk men in hospital blue. It was a dour, even game, settled by a Small goal, and the cup, which was retained permanently by West Ham, was presented by the First Lord of the Admiralty, Mr A. *v.* Alexander. Afterwards the Rovers party had a banquet at the Great Northern Hotel.

On their way to the final Rovers had some notable wins. In round one Rovers were drawn against Bolton and beat them 5–1 at home and 3–1 at Burnden Park. Manchester United were next, and things looked

 Action from the 1940 War Cup Final which Rovers lost 1–0 to West Ham United.

bleak for Rovers after going down 1–2 in the Ewood leg, but they rose to the occasion and triumphed 3–1 at Old Trafford. Sunderland visited Ewood in the third round, but were beaten 3–2. As luck would have it, Rovers were first out of the hat again, and a crowd of 9,742 saw them defeat West Bromwich Albion 2–1. A much larger attendance of 14,238 saw the Rovers beat Newcastle United 1–0 in the semi-final. That goal was enough to send the side to Wembley—a real magic moment at a depressing time, for those able to play.

Rovers' team at Wembley was Barron; Hough, Crook; Whiteside, Pryde, Chivers; Rogers, Butt, Weddle, Clarke and Guest.

Wartime Football

First World War

IN SPITE OF the outbreak of war in 1914, the major football leagues embarked upon their planned programme of matches for the ensuing season, and these were completed on schedule at the end of April the following year. The season saw the club finish fifth, but no-one was particularly concerned, and the Ewood board of directors decided to suspend its activities and not enter the proposed wartime football league.

Having used Ewood Park for schoolboy football during the 1915–16 season, the club staged two friendlies at the end of that season and decided to enter wartime football in time for the 1916–17 campaign. This new game was a poor substitute for a club which, before the outbreak of war, had been one of the top sides in the country.

The war brought to an end the careers of many of the Rovers' championship squad, though the greatest loss to the club was Eddie Latheron. A German shell took the life out of a man who was both one of Rovers' great talents, and an England international at the peak of his career. The wartime game saw a young Harry Healless make his bow before going on to become one of Blackburn's great inter-war stars. It also saw a number of 'old' Rovers come out of retirement,

 Eddie Latheron: killed in the First World War when he was at the peak of his talents.

including Edgar Chadwick, who had played for the Rovers in the days before the Football League!

Second World War

IN CONTRAST to the events of 1914, once war was declared on 3 September 1939 the Football League programme of 1939–40 was immediately suspended and the government forbade any major sporting events, so that for a while there was no football of any description.

The Rovers had opened the season with a 1–2 reversal at Portsmouth, following it with a defeat at Highbury to the only goal of the game. On 2 September they drew 2–2 with Everton at Ewood, and so when war broke out the following day Rovers were bracketed bottom of the First Division. Like most other clubs, they then arranged local friendly matches.

On 30 September the Rovers waited at Ewood for their visitors, Liverpool, and at the appointed time of kick-off there was no sign of their opponents or news of their whereabouts. They eventually arrived, clad in khaki with soldiers' caps and greatcoats, and proceeded to beat Blackburn 5–0. Liverpool's late arrival was due to the fact that the players had to be collected from various army units and, in fact, two of them had been on a twelve-mile route march that very morning!

Then on 7 October the Rovers suffered another 5–0 defeat, this time at the hands of a Huddersfield side whose red jerseys bore two number twos, two threes, two sixes and two nines. Those were the days when a player would turn up for a match in blue overalls, and when, on one occasion, the Ewood groundsman went with the team as trainer.

On 21 October 1939 the Rovers, in common with other league clubs, began regional competitive football.

The outbreak of the First World War had effectively ended Bob Crompton's playing career; now the Second World War brought his managerial days to a premature end. However, he did take the team to Wembley for the 1940 War Cup final, only to see the Rovers defeated 1–0.

In March 1941 the club suffered a devastating blow when Crompton collapsed and died within hours of supervising the team in a match against Burnley. Crompton was not the only loss suffered during the war—Albert 'Nobby' Clarke, who had been a prolific goal-scorer during the championship season, was killed in action.

As peace returned to Europe, Eddie Hapgood, the former Arsenal and England full-back, was appointed the club's manager; the third former England full-back to hold the post.

West Ham United

OF ALL THE CLUBS in the Football League, other than those played in local derby matches, it is probably West Ham United that have provided the Rovers with the most eventful matches.

It was the Hammers that beat Rovers 1–0 to win the War Cup final at Wembley in 1940, but Rovers gained some revenge in 1959 by winning 2–1 on aggregate in the FA Youth Cup final.

Former Blackburn striker John Byrom was just seventeen years old when, in 1961, he scored a hat-trick in Rovers' 3–2 victory at Upton Park. He was on target again with another hat-trick when the teams met at Ewood Park in 1965 and, believe it or not, Byrom scored all three of Rovers' goals in their 3–3 draw at Upton Park in 1966.

It was on Boxing Day 1963 that Rovers inflicted West Ham's record home defeat in the First Division when they won 8–2 at Upton Park. That victory gave rovers a one-point lead at the top of the First Division. However, two days later the teams met for the return fixture at Ewood Park and, as inconsistent as ever, Blackburn proved no match for the Hammers, who won 3–1.

As recently as 1989–90 the teams produced an enthralling spectacle at Ewood Park, where Rovers survived a second-half fight-back by West Ham to win the game 5–4.

Youth Cup

BLACKBURN ROVERS carried off the FA Youth Cup for the first and only time in their history in 1959. Their opponents in the final were West Ham United, whose centre-half at the time was a tall, blonde teenager who had already been blooded in league football—Bobby Moore. The

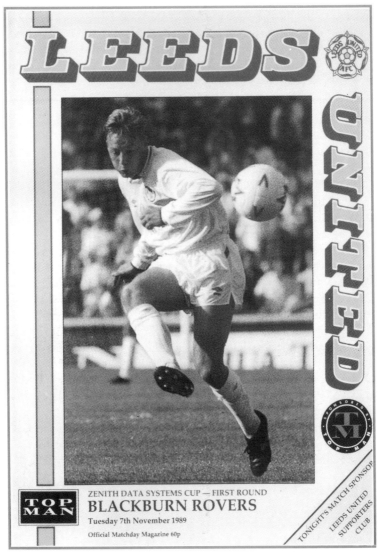

 Programme cover for Rovers' first game in the Zenith Data Systems Cup, 7 November 1989.

first leg at Upton Park was a 1–1 draw and a massive crowd (by today's standards, at least) of 28,500 turned up at Ewood Park to support Rovers' young hopefuls. It was a tense occasion for the youth team nurtured by Johnny Carey and coached by Eric Bell, as the game went into extra time. Paddy Daly scored the only goal of the game to lift the trophy for the Ewood side and send the crowd wild with delight.

Included in the Rovers team that night were Fred Pickering, Keith Newton and Mike England—all three going on to represent their country at full international level.

Zenith Data Systems Cup

THE ZENITH Data systems Cup replaced the Simod Cup for the 1989–90 season. Rovers' first match in this competition saw the club go down to the only goal of the game at Elland Road, Leeds.

In 1990–1 the club entertained Everton, but went down 1–4, with Craig Skinner scoring Rovers' first and only goal in the competition. Because of Rovers' goalkeeping problems at the time, German 'keeper Claus Reitmaier was given a trial game in goal, but it proved to be his only game. Everton's first goal was scored by Mike Newell, now with Rovers, of course. In 1991–2 the club went down again 0–1 to a Martin Foyle goal at Port Vale to go out of the competition in the first round. The club still awaits its first victory in this competition!

Acknowledgements

The author wishes to thank the following for their help in producing this book.

The officials of Blackburn Rovers FC; The Association of Statisticians and the *Lancashire Evening Telegraph*. Thanks are also due to individuals: Colin Cheetham; Peter Bell; Steve Williams; Ian Futter; Chris Brown and George Entwistle. Also to Alistair Hodge and Alan Crosby of Carnegie Publishing for supporting what I hope will be the first in a series on Lancashire football clubs.

List of illustrations

The majority of the illustrations in this book were chosen from the superb collection of photographs held at Blackburn Reference Library, and we are greatly indebted to the staff of the Lancashire Library service for permission to consult the collection and to reproduce some of their material: the photographs of E. Latheron; B. Crompton; D. Shea; J. Simpson; the 'New Grandstand' at Ewood; J. Lewis; A. N. Hornby; the 'original team'; J. H. Forrest; H. Arthur; J. Southworth; J. Brown; F. Suter; W. Davies; W. Townley; Cup Winners, 1884; Cup Winners, 1891; A. Whittaker; League Champions; B. Douglas; J. Marshall; Blackburn Braves, '58; Blackburn Rovers, 1959–60; K. Newton; Blackburn Rovers, 1928; and Blackburn Rovers 1882.

Several illustrations were kindly supplied by the *Lancashire Evening Telegraph*, and we are grateful for the help provided by the library there: Terry Gennoe; Reg Elvy; Johnny Carey; Ronnie Clayton; Bill Eckersley; John Byrom; Mike Newell; Jack Walker; and action from the 1940 War Cup Final.

Finally, thanks to Langwood Ltd, Burnley, for their kind permission to reproduce several front covers from the official programmes which they have published.